# Dog Aggression
## James O'Heare

**BehaveTech Publishing**
Ottawa Canada

Title: Dog Aggression Workbook
Publisher: BehaveTech Publishing, Ottawa Canada.
www.BehaveTech.com
Author: James O'Heare
Cover art and book design: James O'Heare
Copy Editor: Andina Faragher
Illustrator: Jaq Bunn

ISBN 978-0-9738369-3-6

*for Pascale, my loving wife.*

# PREFACE

I'd like to make a few introductory remarks before we get started. First, I would like to dissuade you from thinking there are quick fixes. Finding solutions for dealing with aggressive behaviors takes time and work. Be skeptical of anyone who tries to sell you some one-true-way "method" that works quickly and permanently in all or almost all cases, or one that is alleged to be proven by cutting edge, "groundbreaking" new research (which, in most cases, has not been peer scrutinized or replicated). If you have been watching trainers on TV shows solve problems in half of an hour and spouting on about "discipline" and "dominance" or the quick-fix plan that somehow only they know, then be warned, this is not how it is done. That is entertainment pretending to be professional animal behavior consulting. Professional behavior consulting involves no hype, no TV-show personalities, and no quick fixes. This will be a lot of work, and it requires commitment. The approach in this book is efficient and effective, but it will require you to learn about how this is done and then to apply your knowledge.

Nor will I be providing you with a simple step-by-step recipe. Instead, I will provide you with the tools you will need to understand the particular problem you are dealing with and how to go about changing it. The reason is simple. Behavior is complex. No simple recipe of steps will apply to all cases. What you need is the ability to construct those steps yourself, targeting the specific problem behaviors you are dealing with. You need the flexibility to address not some generic "diagnosis" but your particular problem. And so, what we are going to do here is give you a good, solid introduction to the science and principles of behavior and behavior change programming, outline some important procedures, and describe how you can assess the problem you are facing and apply the principles and strategies to resolving it.

This book is no replacement for a qualified professional. You are the one who faces the ramifications of this problem and you are the one who has to live with this dog, so you need to develop a strong understanding of the topic yourself, but a qualified professional has the skill and experience to help ensure you meet your goals efficiently.

You should maintain a file or a journal as you work through this book. This is a workbook and, as such, it will be interactive. As we work through the book, you will be required to prepare various lists and statements. You will be tracking the frequency of the behavior on a graph and identifying the specific behaviors as well as the environmental context in which they occur. You will want to keep this all in one place and accessible.

I have tried to avoid jargon, but sometimes the best word may be a word you are unfamiliar with. I have tried to define such words when I introduce them. There is a glossary at the back of the book for some of these terms, so if you do not understand a word, check the glossary before you continue. Okay, let's get to work.

# TABLE OF CONTENTS

# CHAPTER 1. INTRODUCTION

If you are reading this book, you are having a problem with your dog behaving aggressively. This book will:

- help you develop a productive perspective on the problem
- help you understand what aggressive behaviors are and are not
- help you understand why dogs perform aggressive behaviors
- show you how to assess the particular problem you are facing, ideally with the help of a professional dog behavior consultant
- help you learn how to construct a behavior change program to address the problem, ideally with the help of a professional dog behavior consultant.

Dogs are no longer simply a tool for hunters or farmers; they are members of our family. Aggressive behavior is distressing for everyone involved; it is both dangerous and detrimental to the social bond between you and your companion dog, not to mention the fact that it reduces the life expectancy for the dog.

## Some Perspective?

Does society really have a "dog aggression problem" as is commonly claimed on TV news shows and elsewhere? If so, how big a problem is it? In this section, I will examine these questions so that we proceed with our exploration of aggressive behaviors in dogs in a rational and grounded fashion.

According to Janis Bradley (2005, p. 15), statistically, dogs are not as dangerous as front-porch steps, kitchen utensils, five-gallon water buckets, bathtubs, strollers, stoves, lamp cords, coffee-table corners, Christmas trees, balloons, or bedroom slippers. Your chance of being killed by a dog, Bradley explains, is approximately one in 18 million, which means you are twice as likely to win the Super Lotto jackpot or five times more likely to be killed by a bolt of lightning. In the United States, children under 10 are killed by caregivers approximately 826 times per year, by buckets 22 times per year, by playgrounds 15 times per year, by balloons 11 times per year, and by dogs approximately 10 times per year. Car accidents kill 43,730 people per year, accidental falls kill 14,440, accidental poisoning kills 14,142, and even bicycles kill 774 people per year, compared with dogs, who kill 16 people per year. For injuries, Bradley reports 7,714,167 caused by falls, 3,990,652 by cars, 3,366,270 by overexertion, 909,688 by "other bites," and 504,627 by bicycles, compared with a mere 340,784 by dogs. More people are hurt each year by slippers, sneakers and other shoes than by dogs, and by tables and chairs, beds and doors than by dogs. And when it comes to severity of dog bites, Bradley reports that the vast majority (92.4%) cause no actual injury, while 7.5% cause minor injury and a meager 0.076% cause moderate to serious injury. Accidental falls cause far more serious and costly injuries, and, in the domestic animal category, horses cause far more medically treated injuries or deaths than dogs. Even cattle cause more deaths than dogs. Taken together, the statistics Bradley presents paint a picture of the "aggression problem" vastly different from many people's perceptions. On a given day, being injured or killed by a dog is vastly less probable than dozens of other potential hazards that we rarely, if ever, become concerned about.

Why is there such hype about the "growing aggression problem" in dogs, when the reality is that dogs almost never kill people, they don't typically bite very often and, when they do, we are rarely injured and, when we are, it is rarely a serious injury? A big part of the problem is the sensationalist way in which the popular media cover the rare stories of dog attacks. Much of our perspective on problems in society comes from the way that these problems are presented on TV and in newspapers. However, the media rarely get the facts straight on dog attacks and tend to exaggerate or embellish their presentation in a way that suggests that dog attacks are a much greater problem than they really are. Sensationalism sells papers and TV advertisement space. Furthermore, as Bradley's research has exposed, much of the statistical work on the scope of the dog attack "problem" is scant, weak or flawed to the point that it gives us a very misleading, if not completely invalid, impression of the true problem.

Society wants to have it two ways with regard to dog behavior. We expect dogs to act like the Littlest Hobo and, when they offer even the most innocuous warning, we are shocked and take great personal offense. We expect dogs to be grateful for our taking them in and caring for them, and refuse to accept that they have likes and dislikes, fears and frustrations, and that they do what works, just as we do. Even though we are much more violent and aggressive as a species, we expect dogs never to be aggressive. If our dogs use aggressive behavior, the shock and sense of betrayal lead us to fear the aggression "problem" and attribute more significance to the incident than is justified rationally. Put in proper perspective, as Bradley (2005) has done, dogs do (though rarely) bite and injure or kill people, but they are not nearly as significant a risk as even slippers or balloons.

For society in general, then, the frequency and magnitude of injuries and death caused by dogs are minuscule. From your perspective, on the other hand, if your dog does develop a tendency to use aggressive behaviors, you are at risk of physical and psychological harm, and the problem is far from minuscule. You love your companion dog. Aggressive behavior jeopardizes your valued relationship, and maybe even your mental health. You may have to decide whether to eliminate the risk by euthanizing the dog, or consider how much effort you are willing and able to devote to changing the behavior. Those statistics we raised are all fine and good generally, but if you are reading this, you are one of the unfortunate people who is already facing the reality of a problem with an aggressive dog. The rest of the book will be dedicated to helping you find solutions.

## What About You?

I would like to take a moment to acknowledge and validate the stress, and in some cases crisis, that can result from facing the reality that your dog behaves aggressively. You probably feel embarrassed and guilty. You probably take the dog's aggressive behaviors personally, as a betrayal of your kindness and trust. You worry that you might not be able to make the necessary changes in her behavior, and you might realize that you have been in denial about it too. You probably feel as though there are few if any options and that the whole thing is outside your control. You also probably feel your relationship with your companion dog deteriorating and experience what is technically a grief process. It would be a challenge not to experience these emotions and thoughts. They are normal responses to a distressing situation.

Please know that you *do* have options—you probably have more options than you realize. Also, know that once you gain a better understanding of the problem, as will be the goal of this book, you will realize that you can exert quite a bit of control over the dog's behavior. If all goes well, I am going to treat you like a dog while you read this book. Before you get upset about that, you should know that I treat dogs better than most people treat each other. I respect that their perspective is legitimate. I try to show them how they can achieve their goals, I try to show them that they have control over their world and thereby empower them, and I try to set them up for success throughout.

Here are some tips for your own behavioral development. Set yourself up for success. Start small and move at a pace that ensures that you succeed, rather than jumping in too quickly and proving that the world controls you instead of the other way around. Focus on preventing the aggressive behavior and on micromanagement until you have a good, solid plan. Write down the problem situations for your dog, and do what it takes to make sure there is no trouble for now. Find rewards for your progress and commitment. You will learn how to graph the frequency of the dog's problem behaviors. Watch that line trend down and recognize that as a reward for your excellent work. Don't try to get too much done too quickly. Set realistic goals. Keep your pace moderate and take setbacks in stride. Find friends and relatives to act as your support network. Talk about your feelings with people you trust who will empathize with you.

I hope this book opens some doors for you and provides some useful tools in your journey.

## Hiring and Working with a Professional Behavior Consultant

Avoid trying to work through a problem with aggressive behavior on your own, even with a good book, advice from experts on email lists, casual advice offered by others in dog parks, or even casual advice from dog trainers. Aggressive behavior is risky. To help ensure that it is resolved as effectively and efficiently as possible, you should enlist the help of a qualified dog behavior consultant who will carry out a proper, formal assessment and help you construct a behavior change plan.

Your first step is to find a knowledgeable and experienced professional who is dedicated to animal-friendly methods. First, I would like to clarify a few terms. Dog trainers are excellent at what they do; they train dogs, mainly in a proactive manner, to perform specific behaviors on cue. Some run group classes, while others work one on one with clients, tailoring the repertoire of behaviors the dog is trained to perform to the lifestyle requirements of the family. Dog behavior consultants, on the other hand, may perform dog-training services, but they are also skilled in reactively helping clients resolve problem dog behaviors.

There are many terms used for dog behavior consultants, some of which are endowed by professional associations or certifying bodies. Basically, the terms used are Veterinary Behaviorists, Certified Applied Animal Behaviorists and Certified Animal Behavior Consultants. Veterinary Behaviorists are veterinary medical professionals with an interest in animal behavior, and usually take a medical model approach to resolving behavior problems (this type of approach is explained on page 13). They are particularly skilled with manipulating the medical/biological contexts for behavior. They may prescribe medication and perform surgeries to help resolve the problem behavior. Unless the problem behavior is predominately the result of medical problems, the Veterinary Behaviorist is not the only answer to the problem. Furthermore, there are very few

Veterinary Behaviorists worldwide. Certified Applied Animal Behaviorists are practitioners certified through the Animal Behavior Society. They have an extensive academic background in ethology, the study of animal behavior. Again, there are relatively few of them, and they are also not the only solution to the problem of aggressive behavior in companion dogs.

Another option is the Certified Dog Behavior Consultants or Certified Animal Behavior Consultants. They are certified through the International Association of Animal Behavior Consultants to be knowledgeable and experienced. You can find a directory of certified members through the association's website at http://www.iaabc.org. Certified Dog Behavior Consultants are particularly skilled, knowledgeable and experienced with working directly with clients to help resolve problem dog behaviors. Their expertise is in resolving companion dog behavior problems and working cooperatively with clients toward that end. Certification—although voluntary—helps assure you that the behavior consultant has a satisfactory level of expertise. Of course, there are many highly qualified behavior consultants who have not sought these voluntary certifications.

Here are some tips on finding a competent professional to work with:

**Visit the web site of professional associations and other directory providers** and look in their directories of members. The most obvious choice is the International Association of Animal Behavior Consultants (http://www.iaabc.org). You can also check the International Institute for Applied Companion Animal Behavior (http://www.iiacab.com), where a directory is maintained of knowledgeable and skilled behavior consultants who are also strongly dedicated to animal-friendly methods. You might also check the directory for the Association of Pet Dog Trainers (http://www.apdt.com) because some professional trainers are also behavior consultants. Alternatively, you could ask your veterinarian for a referral to a Veterinary Behaviorist—this would be most useful if your veterinarian suspects that a medical problem may be the predominant cause of the problem behavior. You could also check with the Animal Behavior Society (http://www.animalbehavior.org) for a Certified Applied Animal Behaviorist. Generally, the Yellow Pages is not a reliable way to find a qualified professional.

**Ask the professional what their credentials are.** A degree in behavioral sciences is good but not strictly necessary, and not always a highly reliable indicator of competence and professionalism. There are very few degrees relevant to consulting with clients on how to resolve aggressive behavior problems in companion dogs, so while a degree in behavioral sciences or a veterinary medical degree is nice, it does not necessarily indicate that the person is competent in applying their knowledge to actual cases. Certification is generally a better indicator of competence and professionalism.

**Ask the professional about their experience** in working with clients with aggressive dogs. They should have years of hands-on experience. Do not necessarily be suspicious of a consultant who cannot offer references, because client identity is held in confidence.

**Ask the consultant about the methods they use.** Ask them if they make use of aversive tools or techniques as corrections for "bad" behavior. These techniques include choke chains, prong collars, shock collars and leash jerks. If they indicate that they do use these types of tools and techniques, even occasionally, this is a red flag that indicates that you should find another professional. Avoid simply asking whether they use animal-friendly methods, as most trainers will indicate that they do, even if they do not or if they use them alongside aversive techniques. Ask specific questions about the tools and techniques described above and throughout this book. Look for the consultant who assures you that they are dedicated to finding creative solutions based on positive reinforcement, that they will change problematic emotional responses where appropriate, and that they will install more acceptable behaviors in place of the problem behavior. And then, ensure they "walk the walk" too.

**Ask them about their theoretical orientation.** It is preferable that a professional wants to focus on identifying the problem behavior, what evokes it and what consequences are maintaining it, rather than postulating "dominance" or trying to label the problem with a "diagnosis" without a full assessment of the actual behaviors involved.

**Pay close attention to whether you feel comfortable with the consultant or not.** They should demonstrate empathy for your situation and make you feel comfortable working with them. Some consultants will be more focused on the problem behavior than on consoling you. That is fine, provided that you feel comfortable working with this professional.

**Observe how the professional interacts with your dog.** It is not necessarily important that they go "goo goo gah gah" over your dog, but they should certainly display respect for the dog. They should ask permission before working with your dog. You should feel comfortable with everything you see them do with your dog and with declining to allow any particular interaction. Never let a professional do something with your dog that you are uncomfortable with just because they are a "professional."

**Ask the professional about how they organize their consultations.** Ask how the professional relationship will work, how much it will cost, what the obligations are of each party and about other details involved in the professional relationship. The consultant should provide clear answers to these questions. It is generally a good sign if they have liability waivers, services contracts and other forms prepared for you to evaluate.

## Roles and Responsibilities of the Guardian and Professional Dog Behavior Consultant

Ultimately, you are responsible for your dog's behavior and the decisions made about resolving it or not. It is common for guardians to attempt to put the responsibility onto the behavior consultant, but in the end, you make the decisions and the consultant helps you do so. The behavior consultant's job is to provide you with information you need to make decisions and to help construct a plan of action you can carry out, sometimes with and sometimes without their hands-on assistance. You are free to choose whichever professional you like, to not hire a professional at all, and to take any, all or none of the advice offered. Along with this choice comes responsibility for the outcomes.

## Liability Issues

Generally, in the United States, people are liable for the damage caused by their dogs, unless the victim was trespassing or committing a felony, the dog was assisting the police or military at the time, the victim provoked the dog, or the person injured was a dog professional who assumed the risk of working with dogs. Other exceptions may exist and would differ from state to state. Most states have a statutory strict liability. Under this system, the dog's guardian is completely responsible for all damages to the victim. It is not required that the guardian be proven to have been negligent, or that they knew the dog might bite, only that the dog did bite. States not adhering to the statutory strict liability system follow the one-bite rule. Under this system, the guardian is not held liable for the first bite a dog commits, but is held liable for any subsequent bites, since the first bite creates a known dangerous propensity of the dog to bite. Under this system, liability is determined by the flow chart in Figure 1.

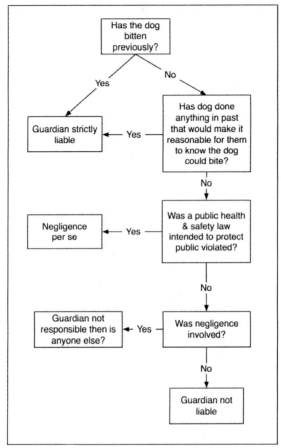

Figure 1. Flow chart for determining liability in states with the one-bite rule

In certain circumstances involving aggressive behavior in dogs, a dog guardian may be found to have committed a criminal offense, and criminal as well as civil action may be taken against them.

Canada is similar to the United States in its dog bite laws, with a few exceptions. For example, in Ontario, the Dog Owners Liability Act (R.S.O. 1990, c. D. 16, s. 1) is a strict liability law similar to laws in the United States, although no exceptions to the guardian's liability are made for trespassers or for those committing criminal offenses.

In the United States, dog bites account for one quarter of all homeowner's insurance liability claims, totaling approximately $345.5 million annually, with an average claim of $16,600 (Insurance Information Institute at http://www.iii.org/). Most states have also passed laws imposing stiff penalties for guardians of dogs who cause serious injuries or death. Some insurance companies require guardians to sign liability waivers for dog bite incidents. Others merely charge homeowners (or renters, or car owners) more for having dogs, or will not provide a policy at all for guardians of dogs that the insurance company considers to have a natural propensity to be dangerous; these might include American Pit Bull Terriers, Rottweilers and others. Some companies require that the dog be taken to classes intended to reduce the odds of aggression or that the dog wear a muzzle in public.

What does all this mean for you? In most cases, it means that you will be held civilly liable and perhaps criminally culpable for any damage caused by your companion dog. You should keep these legal risks in mind when working with your dog.

## Perspectives on Behavior and Changing Behavior

There are many ways to look at explaining, predicting and changing behavior, some more popular than others, and some more efficient and effective than others. Unfortunately, "popular" is not always the same as "efficient and effective." Some people—including many professional animal trainers—choose to use a medical model, which views behavior as normal versus abnormal (disordered). They may speculate about so-called "dominance" that drives the dog's behavior, and they may throw a grab bag of tricks and intuitions at the problem with varying degrees of success. The tides are now turning, and many professionals are taking a more behavioral approach, identifying the actual problem behavior and the events in the environment that maintain it. This approach looks at observable, measurable behavior, the stimuli (i.e., things and events) that evoke it and the consequences that maintain it, not questionable interpretations of it or speculative generalizations that may or may not be correct. The behavioral approach is backed by much research and is more efficient and effective in explaining and changing behavior.

Part of my task in this book will be to help you see behavior through "behaviorist-colored glasses" and help you put inefficient, outdated ideas behind you. This will make your journey much more efficient and effective.

# CHAPTER 2. WHAT IS AGGRESSIVE BEHAVIOR AND WHY DO DOGS AGGRESS?

## What is Aggressive Behavior?

There are many definitions for aggressive behavior, many of which have both strengths and weaknesses. I will define aggressive behavior as attacks, attempted attacks or threats of attack by one individual directed at another individual. Attack behaviors for dogs usually mean bites. By "threats of attack," I mean communication signals that tend to predict that an attack will occur unless the dog achieves what she wants. (Usually what the dog wants is to increase distance between herself and the other dog or person.) In dogs, threats of attack usually refer to growling, snarling and lunging. Other behaviors, such as hard-staring and raised hackles, are also often precursors to attacks. However, since these behaviors are also associated with other situations—including general arousal or stress—it is more of a stretch to consider them aggressive by nature. By "attempted attacks," I include behaviors that would be attacks if they were successful. Snapping might be an attempted attack in some cases, although it is often just a threat. But really, we do not need to get too caught up in definitions; we know aggressive behavior when we see it.

## Why do Dogs Aggress?

In the past, some people have argued that we are born blank slates and that our experiences alone cause our behavior, while others have argued that our behavior is predetermined by our genetic code. It is now known that both nature (genetics) and nurture (experience) contribute to behavior. Our genetics provide us with certain reflexes and some general tendencies, but these can be influenced by learning. Learning also influences our more voluntary, goal-directed behavior. When it comes to nature versus nurture for behavior, you cannot have one without the other.

As a species, dogs (and other animals, including humans) come with a biological makeup that includes the tendency to use aggressive behaviors. Aggressive behavior is adaptive. That is, animals that have made use of aggressive behaviors in specific circumstances have been successful in reproducing and passing their genes on to the next generation, including the genes that allow for aggressive behaviors. By this mechanism, genes associated with aggressive tendencies become more common in the population.

In the context of an individual dog, aggressive behaviors are also often adaptive. Aggressive behavior is just behavior, obeying the same rules as all other behavior. It occurs because it is efficient and effective in allowing the dog to achieve certain goals. There are broadly only two functions for any behavior, including aggressive behaviors:

- to allow the dog to gain access to something
- to allow the dog to avoid or escape something.

We will explore these functions in greater depth below. For now, it is important to appreciate that dogs use aggressive behavior either because they are trying to access something they want, or they are trying to escape from or avoid contacting something they dislike or fear. If you can really internalize this concept, you will have gone a long way to learning how to explain, predict and change dog behavior. I will spend a big part of this book reinforcing these basic principles because they are the key to understanding behavior and changing it.

If a behavior is problematic, you should first look to make sure it is not being facilitated by a medical problem. Once your veterinarian has ruled that out, or taken steps to cure the medical problem involved, you need to look at why the dog is performing the behavior. What is she getting out of it? That is the key question. She may or may not be motivated by problematic emotional responses like fear. Either way, there is something she wants to access or something she wants to avoid or escape.

Some people seem to see all behavior in terms of "dominance." People with this mindset interpret most behaviors as an indication that the dog wishes to be "the boss" or the "alpha wolf" and is staging a coup. They believe that there must be a winner and a loser in every relationship and that each party is naturally pitted against each other to be the winner. In my opinion, this perspective has done nothing but pit guardian against dog in an adversarial relationship. My suggestion, if you are inclined to think in terms of dominance, is to drop it completely. There is nothing helpful in this approach at all. In fact, not only will it promote an adversarial relationship, but it will distract you from the vastly more straightforward approach of identifying the actual problem behavior and the things and events in the environment that are controlling it. There is no scientific support for dominance as it relates to companion dogs and changing their behavior, but there is vast support for the simple principles of behavior as I am describing them here. Dominance is a popular notion, particularly among those who are looking for a hook to sell more books or a new TV show. You'll get nothing good from seeing relationships as win–lose scenarios. Instead, see social relationships as individuals seeking reinforcers (rewards). We are all just doing what it takes to get us what we want. If your dog is aggressing, it is not because she is dominant over you; it is because this has simply proven to be an effective means of accessing reinforcers. Identify those reinforcers, adjust them so that some other, more acceptable behavior is successful, and the behavior will change. How to do this is described in detail later in this book.

Some people may also be thinking that the dog is ungrateful, spiteful or angry. It is questionable whether a dog can be grateful or spiteful. Anger, if dogs experience it, is probably an expression of frustration when they are prevented from gaining access to reinforcers. No-one is plotting to hurt your feelings, and you cannot hold lack of gratitude against a dog. These perspectives are just not helpful. Resist the urge to indulge in them.

## Interpreting a Dog's Communication Signals

It is important that you are able to interpret your dog's communication signals because they help you predict the behavior she will show in the near future. They help you determine whether she is likely to aggress or whether she is fearful. They also help you determine what things in the environment are associated with the aggressive behaviors and how your actions are impacting on the dog. Interpreting a dog's communication signals takes practice.

When interpreting communication signals, it is important to look at the whole dog, not just a single part, and to look for clusters of signals, and not just individual signals. The reason for this is that these signals are complex, and they are constantly changing as the dog's motivations change. There are also often conflicted or mixed signals to deal with. By looking at the whole dog and clusters of common signals, you improve the odds that you are right about what the signals are indicating about the dog's near-future behavior. Furthermore, you should always take the whole context into consideration. A signal or set of signals can indicate one thing in one environment and another in a different environment. So, look at the whole dog, look for agreement among signals and also look at the environment.

Basically, a dog's communication signals can be viewed as agonistic signals, affiliative signals, or mixtures of both. Agonistic signals are signals that involve aggressive intentions or fear/appeasement. Affiliative signals are signals that communicate the intention to engage in prosocial (cooperative, friendly) contact. First, examine the diagram below to see the relationship between these categories of signals.

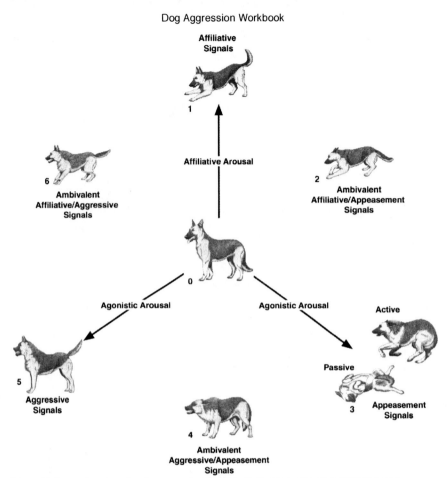

Figure 2. Arousal and postural communication signals in dogs, showing affiliative and agonistic signals, including aggressive behaviors and appeasement signals.

First, look at the dog in the center. This dog is relaxed. As arousal (readiness for activity) rises, signals further from the center will become obvious. You will also notice the conflicted or ambivalent signals between the main categories. Let us look at each category in turn.

## Affiliative Signals

Affiliative signals express the dog's nonfearful and nonaggressive intention to interact in a friendly manner. Simply put, they usually serve the function of allowing the dog to approach another animal. It is important that you can recognize affiliative behaviors so that you can take advantage of the opportunity to reinforce prosocial behaviors, and can distinguish these signals from agonistic signals, often associated with aggressive behavior.

The top position in the diagram (dimension 1 in Figure 2) represents high arousal and the absence of appeasement signals or aggressive behaviors. This position may best be filled by play signals or, under special circumstances (related to season and sex), courtship behaviors. Less aroused affiliative signals could include mutual grooming or a preference for simple closeness.

### Play Signals

Figure 3. Play signals

A dog seeking to interact prosocially will often use invitations to play. These invitations might include play bows, eye flashing (you see flashes of the whites of the dog's eyes), sneezing, panting and a lumbering gait. Such signals may also be used to reassure a playmate during play encounters that play, rather than hostility, is intended. Play between dogs usually takes the form of mock combat or chase-and-be-chased games. The communication signals used during play effectively inform the playmate that the otherwise apparently hostile behaviors are actually meant as play, with no intent to harm. When dogs play, they repeatedly use these signals to minimize misunderstanding.

The play bow is a familiar posture in which the dog bows the front of her body so that her front legs are parallel to the ground, while the hindquarters remain in the standing position. The dog may also offer a few friendly barks to encourage a playmate, usually of higher pitch than barks used during agonistic encounters. While wrestling in mock combat, the dog's eyes will often open wide as she looks sideways at her playmate, resulting in a flash of the whites of the eyes (eye flashing). As most dogs play, they pant and often sneeze. The panting usually oscillates in pitch and is relatively loud. Another sign of play intention, and hence the intention to approach and make contact, is the lumbering gait. This usually occurs when one dog is charging at another dog, or when they are running side by side. They seem to bound, or rock forward and backward as they run. This looks very carefree and easygoing, and is the opposite of the stiff gait of agonistic signals. Playing dogs will take frequent short breaks in which they stand relatively still, looking away from their opponent (these are called cutoff behaviors and are described further below).

### Less Aroused Affiliative Signals

Other affiliative signals can be observed in the relaxed, confident dog outside play situations. These signals are less aroused and subtler than the play signals, again with an absence of agonistic signals. In Figure 2, these signals would be placed in dimension 1, but closer to the center than play signals. Calm, relaxed dogs have relaxed muscles. Their ears are in the regular position for the breed (not forward or held back). Their tail is carried in an easy position, not tucked between their legs or held particularly high (taking into account the normal position for the breed), and may wag gently, if at all. If the dog is more than merely calm and relaxed but also initiating social contact or responding to initiated contact, she may look at the other individual with a gentle pant. Her tongue may hang out (not usually curled at the tip) and bounce gently with each breath. If she is not under stress, her mouth will look relaxed (not pulled back in a forced, wide grin with furrows behind and above the mouth). Her eyes will be soft, and pupils will appear normal, rather than dilated. She may raise a paw, and may even burp in your face (probably derived from food-sharing behavior). There will be a distinct absence of agonistic behaviors.

*Ambivalent Affiliative/Appeasement Signals*

Figure 4. Ambivalent affiliative/appeasement signals

In dimension 2 in Figure 2, signals are conflicted between appeasing and affiliative. Dogs in this category show some appeasement signals (see below), and an absence of any aggressive signals. Some more confident affiliative signals will be used at the same time as some appeasement signals, or else the dog will vacillate back and forth, from more confident affiliative signals to appeasement signals. This is a conflicted state. Most friendly dogs will make use of a few mild appeasement signals (preemptively to avoid hostility), but are not as strongly conflicted as a dog in dimension 2. Friendly (nonplaying) dogs are just slightly to the right of dimension 1 in Figure 2, and usually only mildly or moderately aroused. Cutoff signals (see below) may also be seen in this plane.

## Agonistic Signals

Agonism includes acts of attack, escape, threat, defense and appeasement. Agonistic signals, which may serve various functions, include signals that predict aggressive or appeasement behavior. In practice, most signal clusters are ambivalent, involving signals from more than one dimension at the same time. Nevertheless, highlighting the distinction between signals allows us to appreciate the opposing motivational state of the dog and hence her likely near-future behavior.

### Appeasement Signals

In dimension 3 of Figure 2, appeasement/fear signals are prominent. Appeasement signals indicate a lack of confidence and serve to avoid hostility. The dog may or may not be seeking to interact affiliatively, but most importantly, she is seeking to avoid hostility. These signals are a nonaggressive means of achieving escape or preventing hostile or aversive treatment. Appeasement signals can be either active or passive.

**Passive Appeasement Signals**

Figure 5. Passive appeasement signals

Passive appeasement behavior includes lying in a recumbent position, exposing the underside of the chest and sometimes the abdomen. Presenting the abdomen usually occurs in response to another dog investigating the genital region. The ears are directed back and down, flat against the head, and the tail is held down, usually between the thighs, and often wags slightly. Occasionally, the dog will expel a small amount of urine. She will remain motionless until the other dog has finished her investigation.

**Active Appeasement Signals**

Figure 6. Active appeasement signals

In active appeasement, unlike in passive appeasement, the dog actively enters the other dog's or person's personal space. Active appeasement seems to occur during greetings or after some incident in which a misunderstanding of signals might take place. If an incident occurs accidentally that might communicate a challenge to the other dog, the first dog may use active appeasement signals to prevent the situation moving to aggression. The actively appeasing dog will have a crouched, diminutive posture, with ears back and down close to the head, and tail in a low position, often between the legs. She will often wag her tail, but her whole rear-end will wag rather than just the tail. She may approach the other dog with her body curled in a "U" shape, presenting both her face and her anal area for inspection. She will push her muzzle into the nose or mouth of the other dog and lick with short, repeated laps. Active appeasement signals seem to be modified infantile food-begging responses. These signals look like groveling.

## *Ambivalent Aggressive/Appeasement Signals*

Figure 7. Ambivalent aggressive/appeasement signals

In dimension 4 in Figure 2, the dog is conflicted between using appeasement signals and using aggressive signals in order to increase her distance from the other dog or person. This is the position of the classic "fear biter." The dog will make use of both aggressive and appeasement signals, often vacillating from one to the other. The closer the dog gets to appeasement, the more consistent will be the appeasement signals. As the dog swings closer to the aggressive position, the aggressive signals will become more consistent.

Frequently, this dog will be diminutive (crouched), but more frantic. One of the most reliable indicator signals in this situation has to do with the shape of the mouth. Dogs at the appeasing position rarely show any teeth. Dogs at the aggressive position usually show only their canines and incisors, with the mouth in a tight, forward "C" shape. The ambivalent dog will often have an open, wider "C"-shaped mouth position, showing more of the premolars and molars. The tighter the "C" shape, the closer the dog usually is to the aggressive position. She may start to raise a lip on one side or both and growl. In dogs who are ambivalent between appeasement and aggression, raised fur on the back of the neck or spine (piloerection) often forms a line down the dog's spine. Piloerection indicates arousal. The pupils may dilate. This indicates that activation of the autonomic nervous system—which is responsible for fight-or-flight behavior—is taking place. If this dog cannot escape or make the other animal leave her alone, she may resort to more aggressive signals. She may snarl, lunge, snap or bite.

## *Aggressive Signals*

Figure 8. Aggressive signals

In dimension 5 in Figure 2, the dog does not use affiliative or appeasement signals. Dogs usually make extensive use of threat displays before resorting to actual attack. Generally, a threatening dog appears up and forward, looking as large and powerful as she can, the opposite of fear or appeasement. The hind feet will probably spread more broadly, in anticipation of forward lunging. The tail will ride high and often swing back and forth in a flagging motion or, alternatively, in a quick, almost vibrating motion. Piloerection will be prominent, and the dog will become extremely stiff. The dog will make direct, hard eye contact with the target. As arousal increases, the dog may lower her head, perhaps as a protective measure for the throat. When a dog attacks, she may bite repeatedly, or bite and hold on, with or without shaking. At a slightly lower level of arousal, the dog may put a chin or paw on the back of the other dog's neck or their back. She may mount the other dog or, if the other dog is lying down, she may stand over her, attacking if the other dog attempts to move.

## *Ambivalent Aggressive/Affiliative Signals*

Figure 9. Ambivalent aggressive/affiliative signals

In dimension 6 in Figure 2, the dog is displaying both affiliative and aggressive signals. Dogs displaying very assertive—bordering on aggressive—affiliative signals are conflicted between affiliative and agonistic intentions. They are socially awkward or inept. Behaviors in this category include playing without appropriate signals to indicate "play only," or failing to take even a brief turn as the "victim" in mock combat. In play sessions, it is common for one member to display fewer appeasement signals or to use signals such as placing the chin or paw on the opponent's back, or standing over the opponent, not allowing them to move freely; the dog may become more aggressive or assertive if the other dog does not respond exactly as they wish. These signals may alternate with affiliative signals.

## Conflicted Signals

Common types of conflicted signals arise in situations in which the dog has conflicting motivations. Motivational conflict falls within one of three categories: approach–approach conflicts, avoidance–avoidance conflicts and approach–avoidance conflicts. In an approach–approach motivational conflict, the individual is motivated to approach two different goals, where it is impossible to simultaneously approach both. In avoidance–avoidance motivational conflict, the individual is motivated to avoid two things, where avoiding one tends to result in approach to the other. These two types of motivational conflict are not nearly as common as approach–

avoidance conflict. In approach–avoidance conflict, the individual is simultaneously motivated to approach and avoid the same thing.

In situations of motivational conflict, dogs will show ambivalent signals. If the conflict is with a social group member, the dog may use cutoff signals or displacement activities when she cannot escape, or is motivated to also approach. These categories of signals are described below.

### Ambivalent Signals

Ambivalent signals are merely mixed signals (see Figure 2 at positions 2, 4 and 6). When a dog has both reason to avoid and reason to approach something or someone, she will probably vacillate back and forth between affiliative, aggressive and appeasement signals. At any given moment, the dog may show signals from any of the dimensions in the model. Most agonistic behavior is ambivalent; true high-arousal aggressive behavior would involve immediate attack without hesitation, and true high-arousal appeasement/fear-related behavior would involve immediate flight without hesitation (where possible). The behavior of a motivationally conflicted dog can be a risky situation for a person interacting with the dog because the dog could go either way. If you make a wrong move, the dog could shift to aggressive behaviors. A dog who finds herself too close to someone she wants to avoid may escalate quickly to escape or aggressive behavior. If a dog is showing ambivalent signals, it is advisable to avoid sudden movements, ensure that the dog has a readily available escape route, and ensure that she is not forced to approach any closer.

### Cutoff Behavior

Cutoff behaviors appear to be a conflict management strategy that has the aim of reducing arousal. A dog might use cutoff signals to avoid aggressive encounters in situations where she is seeking social affiliation or to avoid a chase–attack if she flees. Cutoff behavior serves to temporarily break off sensory contact with the other animal, thereby reducing arousal in both animals. Cutoff behaviors are different from appeasement signals in that the dog using the behavior is not showing deference. These signals seem to relax both the signaler and the receiver. In dogs, turning the head or body away or averting the eyes; quick, nervous licking; or displacement activities such as yawning or sniffing the ground can serve as cutoff signals.

### Displacement Activities

During instances of frustration or approach–avoidance conflict, displacement activities are common. Displacement activities are behaviors that are otherwise normal behaviors for dogs, but they are performed out of context. In other words, when a dog faces a highly stressful or unsolvable conflict that results in frustration, she may perform various out-of-context behaviors that may delay or avoid the conflict. In dogs, sniffing the ground or even drinking water can act as displacement activities.

## Greeting Rituals

Greeting rituals are a special class of ritualized behavior, used to convey specific information. When dogs greet each other, even after very brief absences, they will reassess each other with a series of mutual probing displays and assessments. There are three basic greeting ritual patterns: facial–lingual, inguinal and anogenital. Facial–lingual greetings between two dogs involve mutual sniffing and investigation of each other's faces, particularly the mouth and breath. Inguinal greetings involve one individual sniffing and investigating the groin region of another individual. The anogenital greeting involves mutual sniffing and investigation of the other dog's anal and/or genital region.

The greeting routine itself is quite flexible. Most dogs approach each other cautiously in an arc, rather than straight on. Once two dogs have made their initial assessment, one or both dogs will often perform play signals, or they may move on to other activities. Some dogs perform what we might consider intimidating behaviors. They may rest their chin or a paw on the other dog's back or the back of the neck. They may mount the other dog, or, if the other dog lies down, they may stand over them. Dogs with "hostile intent" will often stiffen and growl; they rarely tolerate the other dog moving during this process. The other dog may either remain still until the "intimidator" disengages, use active or passive appeasement signals, or perform similar aggressive behaviors in return. This can result in a blustery display of lunging, snarling, snapping and sometimes biting. Affiliative greeting behavior clusters often include mild preemptive appeasement or cutoff signals, which function to help reduce the chance of being treated in a hostile manner.

When dogs greet people, some variations on the themes outlined above are often seen. The dog will be cautious or confident, social or aloof, or shades in between. The more cautious dog will rarely approach. If she is confident enough to approach, she will use cutoff signals or appeasement signals (active and passive). She may approach wagging her tail so vigorously that her entire rear end wags with it. She may approach with a curved body as if to face the person, but also present her anogenital area for inspection. She will often rub her muzzle up against the person or jump up in order to lick the person's face (particularly the mouth). Alternatively, she may approach very slowly and cautiously with her head down, ears back and tail down. This approach is used by fearful dogs, and the person being greeted should avoid sudden movements or intense interactions until the dog has "warmed up." Some dogs are much more confident and will approach for social contact with few cutoff or appeasement signals. They will simply approach and sniff or seek contact. Many dogs will send ambivalent signals.

## How to Handle Aggressive Signals

The first priority with a dog who may act aggressively is to prevent the dog from aggressing. You can achieve this by making changes to the environment and routines that will make aggressive displays far less likely to occur. This means being aware of the presence of things and events (i.e., stimuli) that may act to evoke the dog's aggressive behavior, and the early warning signals the dog displays.

On occasions when the dog does display aggressive signals aimed at escaping or avoiding something, and your safety is accounted for, generally your best bet is to disengage from the situation early and without fuss. Either remove the problem stimulus from the dog or the dog from the environment (see page 62 for a more detailed discussion of this topic).

Punishing behavior such as growling is a very common practice. However, one of two things is likely to occur if these aggressive signals are punished. The dog may escalate her aggressive behavior in order to defend herself, or she may suppress her early-stage aggressive signals. She may learn not to growl, for example, and the early warning signal of trouble has now been lost. Imagine a dog who does not warn before she bites! I have seen this many times, and invariably it has resulted from punishment of the warning signals. Even if punishment is successful in suppressing aggressive behavior, the function for the problem behavior has not been addressed. The dog has not been shown what to do in that situation, just what not to do. Aversive techniques cause more trouble than they suppress, as a section below explains.

Instructions for facing an aggressive display that is targeted at you are as follows:

Do **not**:

- try to scold the dog

- run away
- scream
- stare directly at the dog
- allow the dog to be cornered.

Do:

- cross your arms
- keep an eye on the dog
- move away slowly to a safe place (without turning your back on the dog). If you move away quickly, the fearful dog may lash out at you, even the deferential one.

Remind yourself that it is normal to take aggressive displays personally. However, the dog is merely behaving in accordance with the way the environment is arranged and what she has learned about the various options available to her. Aggressive behaviors are the normal way for dogs to communicate their intention to escape or avoid something. Whereas we might say, "Please, you are making me nervous, can you not stand so close?" or "Hey, step off, Jack!," dogs cannot do this. Their polite request for increased social distance, when they do not feel that they can easily escape (or attempts to escape have been unsuccessful in the past), is to growl, snarl and snap. I encourage you to see aggressive behavior this way rather than anthropomorphically as an ungrateful betrayal of your trust.

## Stress and Aggressive Behavior

Aggression is often influenced by stress. We are mainly interested in what is causing the stress, but there is value in understanding the stress response itself.

Stress is a nonspecific physiological and neurological response of the body when any demand is placed upon it. The demand does not necessarily have to involve aversive stimulation (unpleasant stuff) to cause stress. Every minute, new demands—both biological and psychological—are placed upon all individuals. Animals respond to these demands physiologically, and these responses require effort and preparation for energy expenditure. This preparation and activation of internal resources constitute the experience of stress. Normal levels of easily manageable stress are often thought of as exhilarating. When stress is intense or long term, it can become detrimental and is referred to as distress. Stress resulting from aversive stimulation may also trigger fight-or-flight mechanisms. These conditions can make aggressive responding more probable.

Distress describes the state of an animal when its biological reserves are not sufficient to meet the biological cost of the stress response. As a result, resources must be diverted away from other biological functions such as growth. Distress is a nontrivial form of stress that is actually harmful. Differences between animals in what constitutes distress are largely determined by features of their individual nervous systems, and these features can be inherited. Some dogs may be genetically predisposed to develop aggression problems.

In 1936, Hans Selye outlined a theory of stress response called the general adaptation syndrome (GAS). The fight-or-flight response, which you have probably heard of, is now considered a part of GAS. GAS involves three phases:

- alarm phase/fight-or-flight response
- adaptation phase
- exhaustion phase.

During the alarm phase, part of the nervous system called the sympathetic nervous system is acutely activated. Shortly after this initial activation, the adaptation phase begins, in which the rapid arousal of the nervous system decreases and a return to equilibrium begins; this phase can take some time to achieve. Finally, the exhaustion phase is the result of the heavy toll taken by the alarm and adaptation phases. Resources become depleted, and the animal shuts down in an effort to conserve energy and recuperate. In other words, the body mobilizes its resources to face an emergency challenge (stress) and then suffers a depletion effect (which can become distress) in order to "pay" for that mobilization.

The course of GAS can also be thought of in terms of the acute phase of fight or flight and the chronic phases of adaptation and exhaustion. I will describe both below.

**Fight-or-Flight Response**

When a dog experiences a sudden or acute onset of stress or fear, the body quickly activates its emergency processes. Various chemicals (neurotransmitters and hormones) are released in the body that will prepare the animal physiologically for an emergency. The heart beats faster, and blood flow is guided away from skin and intestines toward the muscles so that they are ready for action. Some of these arousing processes prime the dog for conflict and aggression. As a result of these processes, the dog may be unable to access behaviors that rely on inhibition, impulse control and previously learned coping mechanisms. This sets the stage for fight-or-flight behaviors such as escape or avoidance. The threshold for aggressive behavior is lowered in dogs under stress.

## Adaptation and Exhaustion

Many dogs stay in a chronic state of stress while they are in the adaptation and/or exhaustion phases of GAS. During this stress response, the body maintains an emergency state for an extended period (often resulting in distress), and depletes itself of valuable resources, including those that affect immune system health, growth and learning. Chronic stress reduces the body's energy expenditure, resulting in lethargy and depression, a compromised immune system and impaired learning ability (and perhaps impaired memory function in old age). The result of continued stress is disrupted sleep patterns, difficulty in thinking clearly, disruption of the rational activity of the mind, oversensitivity to pain, impaired learning, and a lack of ability to experience pleasure. This is classic distress. Research has shown that aggression increases during chronic stress.

## Signs of Stress and Distress

Signs of stress and distress are highly variable. Nevertheless, there are some indications from the dog's behavior that stress or distress may be taking place. Below is a list of potential signs of stress. Some of these behaviors may also function as displacement activities or have other functions. With each, it is important to look at the total package of signs and the context to determine, with any level of confidence, that the signs represent actual stress or distress. Some signs involve an increase in activity and reactivity, while others involve a decrease in activity, or shutting down. In acute stress, the dog goes into full "red alert" mentally and physically. With chronic stress, the dog will shut down.

**Lack of appetite.** Dogs under stress will often refuse food or treats. Context is important: a dog who is satiated because she has just eaten a meal will also refuse treats, and lack of appetite could also represent a distaste for the food offered. In the long term, dogs under chronic stress will eat much less and lose weight.

**Rapid, shallow panting or deep, forceful panting.** Panting is normal for dogs who have been exercising or who are hot, and for certain breeds, but these should be deeper respirations, with a relaxed tongue. During stress (which may, by the way, be caused by excess exercise or heat), the lips will be pulled back in a wide grin, causing furrows in the skin under the eyes and on the forehead. This should be viewed in the context of the situation and other signs of stress.

**Lack of focus and attention.** If the dog fails to respond to cues, she may simply be distracted by a squirrel or some other event. A stressed dog, however, is not ignoring commands. She may not even hear them, let alone feel she can oblige. Tunnel vision and tunnel attention make it impossible for her to respond.

**Sweaty paws.** Dogs get sweaty paws in the same way that nervous people get sweaty palms. When a stressed dog walks on a hardwood floor or in her crate, or steps off the veterinarian's exam table, sweaty paw prints may be seen. This is a result of the body forcing fluid out as part of its physiological defense mechanism.

**Yawning.** This is a very common sign of stress and fairly reliable. Unless the dog is about to settle into a nap, yawning will often represent stress. The yawns tend to be more intense than normal. The dog will usually tuck her chin into her chest and yawn intensely. It is important to look for corroborating signs and context because sometimes a yawn is just a yawn!

**Hyperactivity.** A dog who is acutely stressed may become more active as a defense mechanism. She may look frantic or panicked or her behavior may be interpreted as fooling around or simple hyperactivity. This is the quintessential stress activation, often functioning as a displacement behavior. Dogs cannot maintain this for long before the system is drained, a chronic stress sets in and the dog shuts down and becomes inactive.

**Increased frequency of urination and defecation.** A dog who urinates and defecates more frequently than normal may be suffering an illness, or she may be suffering stress. If she voids inside the house, it may be a house-training issue, or a sign of severe stress. When the body is stressed, it will force fluid from itself. The dog will have an undeniable urge to urinate and defecate. This is one reason why voiding should never be punished.

**Vomiting and diarrhea.** Stress wreaks havoc on the body, and the digestive system is usually the first system to react poorly. There may be many reasons why a dog vomits or has diarrhea, including medical problems. It can also be the result of stress.

**Stretching.** If the dog wakes up from a nap and stretches, she is just limbering up, but if she is in a situation that she finds stressful, then she may be showing her stress. Often when faced with a crowd of people or other dogs, dogs will stretch to relieve stress. Stress tends to make muscles tense, and stretching may be a way to relax tense muscles. It may also be a displacement behavior.

**Shaking as if she just came out of water.** Dogs who are stressed may attempt to "shake off the stress." This is often seen in dog classes and at dog parks. When dogs finish with a tense confrontation, they will often give a shake. This again may be a way to loosen up tense muscles, a self-relaxation exercise.

**Confusion.** A dog who is distressed may act strangely and in a confused manner. Confusion can also indicate a medical problem, such as a seizure or diabetic emergency, so caution must be used in interpreting this behavior as a sign of stress.

**Self mutilation.** The behaviors in this category may include tail biting, or chewing a paw or the flank. There may be many reasons for a dog self mutilating, including a genetic predisposition or medical problems (e.g., allergies). The behavior may have been unknowingly encouraged and rewarded, or may be part of a true compulsive disorder. The dog may have an injury or illness that causes pain in that area. Arthritis in the front hocks area is a common reason for geriatric dogs to lick or bite their front legs, for example. Regardless of the cause, stress is taking place when a dog self mutilates. Many sensitive dogs will direct their stress inward through self mutilation. It may also be a displacement behavior.

**Excessive grooming.** A dog who excessively grooms will usually lick at one particular area, such as the paws, flank, or genitals, and may cause damage to that area. Again, the behavior may result from an injury or illness, or an underlying compulsive disorder. The most likely culprit is an allergy, but stress is another possible cause.

**Excessive sleep.** Some dogs are lazy. For example, Greyhounds or English Bulldogs may be showing a normal level of laziness if they lie on the couch 18 hours a day. Every dog has a different energy level, and so this may be a difficult sign to recognize until after a stress reduction program. Many people notice in hindsight that their dog seemed to be shut down, with no energy, before they started managing the dog's stress level. Shutting down is the quintessential sign of chronic stress. Stressed dogs usually will not experience a satisfying sleep, and this may be one reason why they are always trying to sleep.

**Excessive thirst.** A dog who is drinking more than normal may be suffering an illness (such as diabetes), but may also be showing a displacement behavior in an attempt to ease stress.

**Compulsive or stereotyped behaviors.** When an animal is stressed, certain behaviors can become compulsive. If a dog spends a significant amount of time barking, digging or tail chasing, over a protracted period and without apparent cause, then she may be suffering high levels of stress. These may be strategies used by the dog to keep stress at bay. It could also be displacement behavior, or automatically reinforced behavior (that is, reinforced inside the body).

**Overly reactive.** If the dog cannot relax even under situations when nothing much is happening around her, she may be overly reactive. This may relate to ineffective sleep patterns. Breed tendencies to be naturally reactive must also be taken into account.

**Dilated pupils.** This is related to the activation of the dog's nervous system and indicates significant arousal and stress. It must be evaluated in the context of the ambient lighting.

**Whale eye.** Whale eye occurs when a dog opens her eyes wide and looks to the side, such that the crescent-moon-shaped whites of the eye can be seen. In isolation, whale eye resembles "eye flashing," which is used as a play signal. If whites of the eye are accompanied by other play signals, then it is eye flashing, whereas if they are accompanied by freezing, growling or other signs of stress or aggression, then it is whale eye.

**Stiffness.** When a dog is stressed and aroused, the muscles may become tense and hard, producing a very stiff gait and tail movement.

**Shivering.** Many dogs suffering excess stress will shiver. Context will indicate whether the dog is cold or stressed.

**Displacement activity.** Displacement activity involves behaviors that would otherwise be normal for dogs, except that they are performed out of context, and hence will often seem strange and out of place. If a severely stressed dog is asked to do something, she may perform other behaviors (that is, if her attention can be held for long enough for her to hear the request). Dogs may use displacement activities when they are conflicted or confused. For example, when two dogs are interacting and one dog feels intimidated, she may use behaviors such as sniffing the ground in order to create a pause in the encounter that is acceptable to the other dog. Displacement activities are often used along with appeasement signals.

# CHAPTER 3. PRINCIPLES OF LEARNING AND BEHAVIOR CHANGE

## Introduction to the Principles of Learning

Time to put your thinking cap on. This section is going to have a lot of jargon and some really tough concepts to grasp. I will try to make it as painless as possible.

Why is it important to understand the basic principles of learning and behavior change, and why can't I just give you the step-by-step instructions on how to fix the problem? If you can understand these basic principles, you will be able to apply them to the particular problems you are facing, and to other problems in the future. If I were simply to provide a step-by-step set of instructions, it may not address the specific problem you are facing now and it would be impossible to provide step-by-step instructions for all possible problems (we would be trying to jam square pegs into round holes). If, on the other hand, I can arm you with an understanding of these basic principles of learning, as well as strategies and procedures for applying these principles to change problem behavior, you will be able to understand the problem behaviors you are working with and decide— ideally with the help of a professional behavior consultant—how to change them. We will not be trying to jam square pegs into round holes, labeling the problem as though it is a disease, as in the medical model approach. Instead, you will describe the specific problem behaviors your dog is performing, and why she is performing them, and that will imply how to change those behaviors. There is a systematic approach to addressing the problem, but it will require you to apply some basic principles to the particulars. The great thing about grasping these principles is that you can be flexible in applying them to any behavior. Nothing will be a mystery that only a professional can figure out. You will be able to look at any problem behavior and systematically identify why it is performed, and hence what you need to change in the environment to change that behavior. These principles of learning are the basis both for understanding and explaining behavior and for changing it. So, let's jump right in.

## What is Behavior and Learning?

Most simply, behavior is any movement that an animal performs. Usually, in the context of changing problem behaviors, we want to avoid interpretations of behavior or speculations about private mental experiences the dog might be having, and so we differentiate behavior from these other things. Rather than interpreting the behavior, try to get into the habit of describing observable, measurable, discrete behaviors. The dog is not "dominant," for example; rather, the dog performs specific behaviors. The label "dominant" in place of a description of the behaviors does no one any favors, least of all the dog, who, as we have learned, is merely doing what works to access the things she wants. Nor is the dog spiteful. Some of these "feelings" are possible or even probable, but they do not help us in our present endeavor. Some behaviors are easier than others to identify. Some are large-scale, goal-directed behaviors like biting. Others can be involuntary reflexive responses, such as the various physiological occurrences that take place during stress.

Learning is an enduring change in behavior due to experience. There are different types of learning, as described below, but in all instances, the change in behavior results from experience with the environment. You cannot have behavior independent of the environment.

Two types of learning are respondent conditioning and operant conditioning (conditioning is just another term for learning).

## Respondent Conditioning

You've probably heard of Pavlov's dog. Pavlov found that he could condition a dog to salivate in response to a stimulus that had previously been meaningless (neutral) to the dog. He could use a metronome to make a sound, and the dog would drool reflexively. Pavlov achieved this by repeatedly presenting the neutral stimulus (the metronome sound) immediately before food. Food, unlike the sound, is meaningful already. Drooling in response to food is a reflex; it's involuntary. When a dog gets food, she drools. If you present a neutral stimulus immediately before the food, which elicits the drooling, eventually the dog will drool when you present the previously neutral stimulus on its own. This is respondent conditioning.

You're probably wondering why this is important. It is important because emotions involve respondents (i.e., reflexes). Emotional behavior is actually a package of reflexes and more goal-directed behaviors that are motivated by the emotions. For example, fear involves the release of various neurotransmitters in the brain and hormones into the bloodstream. This creates things like narrowed tunnel vision and churning stomach sensations, and these reactions motivate the dog to act; they trigger the fight-or-flight mechanism. The emotion of fear motivates much aggressive behavior; it makes escape and avoidance highly rewarding (I'll use the proper term "reinforcing" in place of rewarding from here forward). Through respondent conditioning, these emotional behaviors can also occur in response to a stimulus that was previously neutral. Just as a dog can be conditioned to drool to the sound of a metronome, she can be conditioned to release these problematic neurotransmitters and hormones that create fearful behavior in response to various stimuli that were once neutral. For example, if a dog has some unpleasant experience in the presence of another dog or in your presence or when she is wearing a particular collar, she may in the future have the same emotional response elicited by those things. This is all automatic; the dog has no choice, just as with drooling when she smells food. This is how emotional reactions are conditioned (learned).

As you can see, respondent conditioning is important because this is the process by which many emotional responses are conditioned to new stimuli, and aggressive behaviors are often motivated by emotional responses. When a stimulus elicits problematic emotional responses, we need to identify that relationship and change it.

That was a lot to take in. Let me restate it more concisely as a review. Reflexive responses, including those that contribute to emotional responses like fear, can be conditioned—they can come to be elicited by things that previously did not elicit them (how does the mere sound of a dentist's drill make you feel?). If a dog associates some unpleasant experience with something else, like strangers in general or choke chains or hands or particular rooms, then it is likely that those things will then also elicit fear in the future. Fear motivates escape and avoidance behavior, which often involves aggressive behaviors, particularly when flight is not likely to be successful. When fear is a motivating force behind aggressive behaviors, we need to find out what elicits the fear and we need to change that emotional response.

## Operant Conditioning

Operant conditioning is another form of learning. Instead of dealing with reflexes (including emotional responses), though, operant conditioning is all about voluntary, goal-directed behavior. This type of behavior is influenced by its consequences. When a dog lunges, bites, snarls or snaps, these behaviors are not reflexes; they are voluntary, goal-directed behaviors, or operants. They may be motivated by emotional responses, but the voluntary behaviors themselves are operants. The most important thing to remember is that dogs, like the rest of us, do what works to get them what they want. It is as simple as that. In the previous section, we addressed changing what the dog wants by changing emotional responses, but now we look at the other part of the dog's behavior—changing what works. Let's look more closely at this type of conditioning, since aggressive behaviors are primarily operants.

## The ABCs of Behavior

In the science of behavior, the relationship between a behavior and the environment that influences it is referred to as a contingency. The most basic elements of this relationship can be remembered easily by their acronym ABC. A stands for antecedent; B stands for behavior; and C stands for consequence. Let's look at the ABCs of behavior a little more closely.

Antecedents are what come before the behavior. They make the behavior more or less likely to occur. They include the stimuli that indicate to the dog that a given behavior will probably result in a particular consequence. Antecedents can include the immediate "trigger" that evokes the behavior, as well as the motivational forces for the behavior (including fear responses that we discussed above).

Behavior is the observable, measurable actions that are evoked by the antecedents. Operant behaviors are voluntary, goal-directed behaviors that operate on their environment to get the dog what she wants. Remember to avoid interpretations and labels as much as possible. Stick as closely as possible to specific, measurable behaviors.

Consequences are what happen after the behavior. Anything that happens right after a behavior that results in the behavior becoming more or less likely in the future is a consequence.

So, basically, the *antecedent* sets the occasion for the *behavior*, which results in *consequences*. All together, this is referred to as a contingency, or the ABCs of behavior. Next, let's try to understand the consequences in particular, since these are what drive behaviors.

## The Contingency Table

The contingency table can help us visualize the consequences that influence behavior. As you can see in Table 10, there are four outcomes for behavior that can influence the frequency of the behavior. You can increase or decrease the probability of a behavior. And you can achieve either of these possibilities by adding or removing a stimulus. This can be a tough notion to grasp, so have a really good look at this table. I will address each in turn.

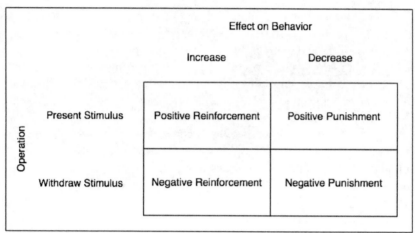

Table 10. Contingency table

## Increasing the Frequency of Behaviors

Reinforcement is what drives behavior. The two categories of reinforcement described below (positive reinforcement and negative reinforcement) are the only two functions for aggressive behaviors. The aggression problem you are working on is maintained through one of these two processes.

### Positive Reinforcement

Positive reinforcement is defined as follows:

1. Performance of a behavior ...
2. followed by presentation of a stimulus ...
3. results in an increased future probability of that behavior.

In other words, you present "good stuff for dogs" after a behavior and the dog is more likely to do it again. When the dog sits and you give her a treat, she is more likely to sit again in order to access the treat.

When a behavior increases in frequency due to the presentation of a stimulus, the behavior has been positively reinforced. Positive reinforcement is the only consequence that does not involve the use of an aversive stimulus—that is, an unpleasant stimulus that the animal acts to escape or avoid. Positive reinforcement is the cornerstone of an effective procedure for changing behavior effectively and efficiently, while avoiding unpleasantness.

Positive reinforcement can maintain aggressive behavior, although it is rare in comparison with the next category we will discuss: negative reinforcement. If a dog aggresses in order to gain access to something (pleasant) then the aggressive behavior is being maintained by positive reinforcement. Look carefully at what follows the aggressive behaviors. Most serve to allow the dog to escape or avoid something, but in some cases, dogs will learn that aggressive behaviors are the most effective way to get what they want. Some people might interpret this as "dominance," but this is not a particularly helpful way of seeing it. It is much simpler to appreciate that we all do what works to get us what we want. If aggressive behaviors work, dogs will use them. Examples of this might include instances where guardians give treats to their dog or pet her when she barks and lunges at people. This is usually with the intention of distracting the dog from the target or counterconditioning a different emotional response (see page 61). In these scenarios, we can predict that the dog will learn to perform these aggressive behaviors in order to get the treats or petting. Dogs are not stupid; they learn quickly what gets them good things. Always look at what happens after a behavior and at the frequency of the behavior. There you will find a contingency that is supporting that behavior. Avoid your preconceived notions and look at the frequency of the behavior and the consequences it produces to figure out why a behavior is being performed.

### Negative Reinforcement

Negative reinforcement is defined as follows:

1. Performance of a behavior ...
2. followed by removal of a stimulus ...
3. results in an increased future probability of that behavior.

In other words, you remove "bad things for dogs" if they perform some behavior and they'll be more likely to use that behavior again. If, for example, you expose a dog to something she fears and only allow her to escape from it if she performs some specific behavior, then you are likely to see more of that particular behavior in the future.[1]

---

[1] Some trainers use negative reinforcement to change aggressive behaviors. They present the feared stimulus in a graded, incremental manner. The dog may or may not aggress, but they allow the dog to escape if, and only if, she performs prosocial behaviors. There is no guarantee with this approach that the dog is not merely learning to put on a friendly face (so to speak). It is possible that we have not in fact

When a behavior increases in frequency due to the withdrawal of an unpleasant stimulus, the behavior has been negatively reinforced. Negative reinforcement involves an aversive (unpleasant) experience—you can't remove something unpleasant unless it was presented to begin with. Note that, even though the word "negative" is used, this only refers to something being removed—it is not a value judgment. Remember, negative reinforcement involves removing something, and the behavior then increases in likelihood.

Negative reinforcement is the most common consequence maintaining aggressive behaviors. Escape or avoidance behavior is maintained by negative reinforcement. The dog will be more likely to perform the behavior if it serves to allow her to escape a scary situation she is in or to avoid that situation once she learns to anticipate it. Usually, a dog will learn escape behaviors first and then, once she can predict the scary situation, she can aggress in order to avoid getting into it to begin with. If aggressive behaviors are effective in getting the scary thing to leave or allowing her to get away, then that strategy will be used again. So, for example, if aggressive behaviors are successful at convincing the postal carrier to leave, or to get a stranger to stop approaching or move away, or to get you to stop approaching the dog's food dish, then the aggressive behaviors are being maintained by negative reinforcement. Ask yourself in all cases, what is the dog getting out of this behavior? When negative reinforcement is involved, she is getting to avoid or escape something; she is convincing the other individual to leave her alone or stop doing what they are doing. Some part of their encounter ceases or is removed.

---

addressed the underlying emotional response. The fear may remain, and reliability is an open question. Negative reinforcement also necessarily involves presenting an aversive stimulus, which may in some cases result in problematic side effects. Furthermore, negative reinforcement is only as reinforcing as the aversive is unpleasant, so this means that the procedure will be either ineffective or highly unpleasant (neither option is ideal). Some trainers claim that this is a nonaversive approach, but this cannot be accurate. While there are varying degrees of aversiveness, and a graded approach ensures it is less aversive than some other approaches might be, if we are talking about implementing an effective negative-reinforcement-based approach, then we are indeed talking about using aversives—that is, using "unpleasant things for dogs." If it was not rather aversive, it simply could not work. Generally, I suggest you maintain a healthy skepticism regarding negative-reinforcement-based procedures (and, in fact, any procedure that involves "unpleasant things for dogs") if anyone suggests them to you, and stick with positive reinforcement, which does not involve any aversive stimulation—no "unpleasant things for dogs." At the time of writing, there are no published, peer-reviewed research articles demonstrating the effectiveness of these procedures on aggressive dogs, although we will probably start seeing some soon, and certainly there are no studies exploring the long-term ramifications of this approach on the dog beyond the specific target behavior. Much research is needed to explore the various angles of this approach and compare it with other less aversive methods, and a process of academic debate and analysis must take place before we can really know much about its advisability. That will take more than a couple of articles; it will take time and, until then, positive-reinforcement-based approaches are probably the best approach to take.

## Decreasing the Frequency of Behaviors

When a consequence results in a decrease in the frequency of a behavior, punishment has taken place. Punishment, including both the categories below, does not drive behaviors in the sense that reinforcement does. Punishment serves to suppress a behavior, but reinforcement is what was driving that behavior to begin with. Unless you control the reinforcement that was driving it, punishment will not be successful in the long term. In fact, if you removed the reinforcement, then you would not need punishment. People are very fond of punishment because it is so intuitive (and aggressive), but the secret of behavior change programming is that reinforcement, not punishment, drives behavior.

### *Positive Punishment*

Positive punishment is defined as follows:

1.  Performance of a behavior ...
2.  followed by presentation of a stimulus ...
3.  results in a decreased future probability of that behavior.

In other words, make "bad things for dogs" happen immediately after a behavior and the dog will suppress that behavior.

When a behavior decreases in frequency due to the presentation of a consequence, the behavior has been positively punished. Positive punishment involves aversive stimulation (unpleasantness). Things that are commonly used as positive punishment include yelling, hitting, "correcting" with the leash and spraying fluid at the dog. Positive punishment can include anything that you do to the dog that they experience as unpleasant. It can result in problematic side effects (explored below). These side effects include a lashing-out kind of aggressive behavior (called respondent aggression), disruption of the social bond between you and your dog, and countercontrol.

Countercontrol means that the dog learns to work around you or otherwise manipulate you in order to avoid the punishments. Positive punishment often leads to further escape/avoidance behavior, commonly resulting in the dog's use of aggressive behavior, which often then becomes negatively reinforced; that is, when the dog uses aggressive behavior, she is successful in making the punishment stop. This is a vicious cycle that often results in the aggression problem becoming worse. It may ultimately lead to euthanasia for the dog and psychological trauma for the guardian. When aggressive behavior is temporarily suppressed by positive punishment, the behavior of the person administering the punishment may also be negatively reinforced; that is, the person learns that punishment of the dog is successful (in the short term) in stopping the dog's aggressive behavior. This creates an unfortunate cycle of the person and the dog manipulating each other back and forth: countercontrol.

Positive punishment might seem like the most intuitive action to take, but it is fraught with insidious ramifications. Fortunately, there are much more effective strategies for changing behavior in most cases—a constructional approach that we will explore below.

### Negative Punishment

Negative punishment is defined as follows:

1. Performance of a behavior ...
2. followed by removal of a stimulus ...
3. results in a decreased future probability of that behavior.

In other words, you remove "good things for dogs" following a behavior and the dog avoids that behavior in future.

When a behavior decreases in frequency due to the withdrawal of a stimulus, the behavior has been negatively punished. Negative punishment involves an aversive experience because it involves an unpleasant event. However, negative punishment—if carried out properly—is usually not nearly as aversive as positive punishment or negative reinforcement. It produces less emotionality and fallout (side effects).

The time-out procedure that is commonly used for dealing with a child's temper tantrum is an example of the application of negative punishment. Another example of negative punishment is playing and delivering treats to the dog and then, when the dog performs a behavior you want to negatively punish, you turn away, staying quiet and motionless, and fail to deliver treats for several seconds. Assuming that the social attention and the treats are pleasant for the dog in that situation, removing them when the dog performs the problem behavior motivates the dog to not perform that behavior, in order to avoid losing your attention and the treats.

## Extinction

Unlike the consequences described above that make up the four quadrants of the contingency table, extinction is the *absence* of reinforcement where it existed before. Remember, reinforcement drives behavior. If there is no reinforcement available for a behavior, there is no reason to perform the behavior. If the behavior doesn't work, the dog won't bother performing it.

Operant extinction is defined as follows:

1. Previously reinforced behavior ...
2. followed by withholding (not removal) of the reinforcers that were maintaining the behavior ...
3. results in reduction in the frequency or magnitude of the behavior.

Don't confuse extinction with negative punishment. Extinction involves withholding reinforcement, whereas negative punishment involves removing a reinforcer that was present.

Besides causing a decline in behavior, extinction procedures have a number of other effects. Think about it. If you usually perform some behavior in order to gain access to a reinforcer and all of a sudden that behavior does not deliver any more, what do you do? Let's say you press the button for the elevator and it does not come soon. Do you simply walk away? That's not usually your first response, is it? Usually you will press the button again, this time maybe a little harder, or several times in a row. Maybe you even press another button, and you may even kick the door if it does not come soon. Similarly, if putting money in a soft-drink machine does not get you the drink, you may click other buttons or give the machine a little shove to shake loose the drink. One final example: you pull the slot machine bar and no money comes through. Do you stand up and walk away? No, of course not. You put another coin in and pull the bar again.

Life is dynamic, and everything does not always work exactly the same way. Sometimes getting access to the reinforcer you seek requires you to perform the behavior again, or perhaps a slightly different behavior. Giving up too easily is not adaptive; you can't get through life successfully with a few simple behaviors and giving up the instant one does not work. So, when you first start using an extinction procedure with your dog, you can expect that initially the behavior will become more frequent or more intense. It will gradually become less frequent and intense as the dog learns that nothing works to get back the reinforcer and she is wasting her time. Do not give in when the behavior initially becomes worse! This will create a bigger problem than you had before. Hang in there. You can also expect increased variability in the behavior. If growling no longer works, then perhaps snarling, or snarling with a lunge, or snapping, or just growling louder, might work. This effect will dissipate with time as long as you remain consistent with the extinction procedure. Finally, you will also find that, as the behavior extinguishes, every now and then the dog will try it again. This is the "just checking" effect. The behavior worked in the past so they may give it another shot every now and then. With continued extinction, these effects will become less frequent. So, expect an initial increase in intensity and variability and the occasional "just checking" behavior and work through it.

Extinction is frustrating for the dog and can therefore result in unwanted side effects (fallout; see page 85). The emotional reaction of frustration can set the stage for emotional behavior. If that elevator does not come after an extended period, you may kick the door before the button-pressing behavior is finally extinguished and your behavior switches to heading toward the stairs. The emotional reaction may set the occasion for increased irritability and an increased probability of responding aggressively to other stimuli that would otherwise be only slightly irritating. Extinction procedures can result in a lashing-out type of aggression, particularly when no alternative source of reinforcement is readily available as a replacement. Extinction is not harmless and should not be used on its own, only as part of a protocol that shows the dog how to access those reinforcers in some other way. In behavior change programming, extinction should only be considered for aggressive behaviors that are maintained by positive reinforcement, and only in conjunction with training the dog to access the reinforcer using another, more acceptable behavior instead.

## Variables Influencing Operant Conditioning

To maximize the effectiveness of operant conditioning, you have to meet a few conditions. This applies both to conditioning that takes place without your participation and to training your dog or changing her aggressive behaviors. The conditions are:

- immediacy
- contingency
- motivating operations
- individual differences
- magnitude.

The more immediate are the consequences, the more likely they are to work. If you wait more than even a few seconds, the conditioning may be weak, if it occurs at all.

Contingency (in this context) means that the behavior is followed by the consequence, and that consequence does not occur unless the behavior occurred first. Contingent consequences tend to strengthen conditioning, whereas noncontingent (willy nilly) consequences tend not to strengthen conditioning. The more times the behavior and the consequence are noncontingent, the less likely conditioning is to occur.

Motivating operations refer to how much the dog wants to access a consequence or wants to avoid a consequence. If she is satiated (full of treats, for example), then treats will not be that valuable and she will not work as hard for them. If, on the other hand, she is deprived of food, then she will be hungry and more likely to work for treats. Of course, I am not advocating starvation at all; perhaps just training before meals rather than after.

Between individuals, there is wide variation in how valuable a particular consequence will be. It is important to keep these individual differences in mind when working with animals.

Magnitude refers to the amount of a consequence. Generally, the greater the magnitude of a consequence, the more effective it is as a reinforcer or punisher. An animal will be more likely to respond for a bigger reinforcer than a smaller one, and will be more likely to discontinue a behavior for a bigger punisher than a smaller one. Also, more frequent but smaller treats are generally better than less frequent but larger treats.

## Operant–Respondent Interrelationships

It is important to note that both operant and respondent conditioning are always taking place. These are not just things that occur when you are training or when the dog is aggressing; they each take place all the time. Consequences are always following behaviors; those behaviors are always either remaining stable, increasing or decreasing in likelihood; and behaviors are always taking place in the presence of various stimuli that will more or less come to evoke them. Respondent conditioning is also taking place on an ongoing basis. In terms of emotional responses like fear and joy, dogs are always experiencing emotions of various intensities and they are always learning which stimuli in the environment predict them. What will elicit any given emotional response is always being maintained, strengthened or weakened.

This has some important implications for your work. Always be aware that, for voluntary behaviors, what follows the behavior may increase or decrease its likelihood in the future, strengthen or weaken it. When it comes to emotional responses, we need to make sure that, if possible, we promote pleasant or joy-related emotions, particularly in circumstances that have previously elicited fear. Unpleasant experiences will become associated with what is going on at the time. If you make use of harsh punitive techniques or even if you simply allow the dog to have unpleasant experiences, she will associate that experience with the common factors in the environment. That could be other dogs, a particular collar or a location, and it can particularly mean you, the handler. If you are present each time the dog experiences fear, then you will come to elicit fear, which is obviously not good for your relationship. Dealing with problematic emotional responses is tricky business, so your goal is to minimize the frequency with which they occur, the intensity of them, what will come to reliably predict them and, of course, what kinds of consequences follow the behavior the dog uses to escape or avoid something. Always think about what consequences are affecting behaviors and how emotional responses are being conditioned.

Now that we have a good introduction to the basic principles of learning, we can proceed to details on how to carry out a formal assessment of aggressive behavior. Following that, we will explore behavior change procedures and how to put all of this together to construct your plan of action.

# CHAPTER 4. ASSESSMENT

Now it's time to do a formal assessment of the problem. This is something you should ideally work on with a professional. There are different types of assessments. Perhaps the most common type performed these days is based on a medical model. In this assessment style, behavior is seen as pathological or abnormal and the behavior is "diagnosed" by labeling the problem with a term in one of many classification schemes. For example, it might be labeled as dominance aggression, possessive aggression or territorial aggression. This system uses broad, generic terms to describe the problem you are facing, and it is usually hit or miss (as most broad generalizations are). The medical model is appropriate for medical conditions but not for behavior. Far more efficient and systematic is to take a behavioral approach. In a behavioral approach, we do not apply generic labels—instead, we systematically identify the *specific* problem behaviors and their relationship to the environment. That means describing the specific problem behavior and identifying the antecedents (things that come before the behavior) and the consequences (things that come after the behavior). Once we understand exactly what the specific problem behaviors are, what evokes them and what maintains them, we are in an excellent place to adjust the environment, which in turns adjusts the behavior. See how much more reasonable this is? It is specific to the problem you are experiencing rather than a broad generalization, and it is systematic and research based rather than a grab bag of intuitions and guestimation. The behavioral assessment is called a functional assessment.

Of course, sometimes, medical conditions contribute to behavior problems. In such cases, behavior is still behavior and not a disease, but the medical condition acts as a type of antecedent, making the problem behavior more likely and affecting how reinforcing a particular consequence will be. So, before any behavioral assessment is carried out, you must have your veterinarian perform a full checkup on your dog, including any necessary tests. We can never be sure we have ruled out contributions from medical problems, but your veterinarian can help reduce the odds that a medical problem is contributing to the behavior. If a medical condition is identified, this condition should be treated as appropriate. You must be sure you understand the nature of the medical condition and how it might affect your choices regarding how to address the behavior itself.

# What is a Functional Assessment and How Do I Do One?

A functional assessment seeks to identify the function for a given behavior: why is it being performed? Professional behavior consultants making use of a behavioral approach will have extensive knowledge of how to carry out this assessment. I will briefly describe parts of the process here so that you can understand the process and come to understand better the problem behaviors you are dealing with, but it is best to work with a professional behavior consultant on this.

First, a word on quantifying behavior. Before, during and after a behavior change program, you should track the incidence of the problem behaviors, ideally on a graph. This will help you determine objectively whether you are meeting your goals and whether the program is working or in need of adjustment. The vertical axis of the graph can represent the frequency, duration or intensity of the behavior. Usually, you want to know how often it is occurring in a given time period, but in some cases, it is more important to know how long the behavior was performed for, or how intense it was. Measuring intensity can be tricky and is rather susceptible to error because you will usually be making a judgment call, and your criteria may change as time goes on. In any case, choose the dimension you want to measure for the vertical axis.

The horizontal axis often represents time, such as days, or perhaps hours. In some cases, the horizontal axis may represent instances of contact between the dog and the stimulus that has provoked aggressive behaviors in the past. This might be a more useful approach when you are taking steps merely to avoid the situation rather than using a behavior change technique. In that case, the decline in frequency tells you about the relationship between the dog's behavior and the stimulus and not about your avoidance of the problem. Note that if you measure with respect to instances of contact, your frequency on the vertical axis will be 0 or 1 in most instances; the aggressive behavior either occurred or it did not. Choose what is most informative for your particular case.

Once you have set up the graph, place a dot at each time point or instance (on the horizontal axis) to mark the appropriate frequency, duration or intensity (on the vertical axis). Continue to monitor the behavior in this way throughout your work on the problem. Make a vertical line to indicate where you made specific changes to the dog's environment. For example, if you have been tracking the behavior and you then implement a behavior change program, draw a vertical line at the time where you implement the change. This way, when you are looking at the graph, you can see what has happened to the behavior when you make specific changes. See the example graph below.

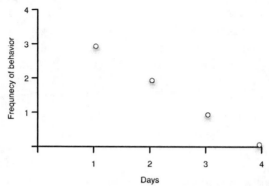

Figure 11. Example of a graph to track a problem behavior. In this case, the frequency of the behavior is measured for each day. On day 1, there were 3 instances of the behavior and on day 2, there were 2 instances. The trend is tracking downward each day in this example, meaning the behavior is becoming less frequent each day.

Our goal in assessment will be to develop an accurate "contingency statement." A contingency statement is a single sentence (sometimes more if necessary) that states, in plain English, what the antecedent, behavior and consequences are for the problem you are facing. Here is an example of a contingency statement:

> When a stranger approaches Fido within 6 feet while she is eating from her food dish at home, Fido will freeze and growl, and if the stranger approaches to within 3 feet, Fido will lunge and bite the stranger in order to prevent their approach.

In this case, we have two sets of behaviors and antecedents. Antecedent 1 involves strangers approaching Fido to within 6 feet while she eats from her dish at home. Antecedent 2 is the same but involves a distance of 3 feet rather than 6. You can include them together as long as they are clear, otherwise you should divide them into separate statements. Notice how specific this is. It is not just anyone, it's strangers, and it's not just anywhere, it's at home. It is also not just at any time or in any context but while she is eating and also from her dish. Each of these is what we call a necessary condition; each element must be present as a package in order to provoke the dog to freeze and growl. If strangers approach to within 3 feet, lunging and biting will be evoked. There can be the occasional exception, but generally, this is the controlling antecedent that gets the behavior to take place.

Notice that the behaviors described in the contingency statement are specific. The statement does not refer to spite, jealousy or dominance, or even to territory or "guarding," but rather to specific, observable behaviors that we could measure and count. Notice too that freezing and growling are combined here. In this case, they always occur together (they are controlled by the same antecedents and consequences), so it is useful to identify them as a package. Separated from freezing and growling are lunging and biting, which are controlled by the same consequence but evoked by a different antecedent (3 feet proximity rather than 6). And notice that rather than a broad, uninformative generalization, we have a specific description of the problem you are dealing with and a statement about why it is occurring.

The consequence of the aggressive behavior in this example is to keep strangers away from Fido and her food while she is eating. That's about all we can determine for sure in most cases. We don't know what she is thinking; we just know that, in the past, this has been the actual outcome for the behavior. Given that this has been a consistent outcome, we can reasonably infer that it is what is maintaining the behavior. We could test it experimentally, but if it is reasonably clear what consequence is maintaining the behavior, the test will be part of our behavior change program (if the behavior does not decline when we apply the program, we can suspect we were wrong about the consequence in our assessment). But for now, let's try to keep it simple and leave the complexities for the professional animal behavior consultant.

How do we determine what the ABCs are? Start with the behavior. Write down the specific, observable, undesirable behaviors. Write them all down, perhaps in rank order from most to least problematic. If some always occur only together in a package or sequence, clump them together, but still write each one out.

Now that you have a behavior to track, start quantifying it. Prepare your graph and try to act normally (with safety precautions, of course) for, say, ten occurrences of the behavior or a week or two. You might need to change the variables in your graph as you develop a better understanding of what affects the behavior, and that is fine. If, in your case, it is unacceptable to allow ten occurrences of the behavior (as will be the case in many instances), don't wait before instating your behavior change program. Start right away with the program and the graphing. At least you will be able to see the trend; that is, whether it is remaining stable, going up or going down. Also, write down now what you believe are the antecedents and consequences. But remember, be open to the possibility that you might be wrong and may have to adjust these ideas. Continue reading for details on how to identify the antecedents and consequences.

For now, write down your initial thoughts on what you remember from the past about what usually comes before and after the behavior.

As you track the behavior, take notes on the antecedents. When the behavior occurs, note what was going on immediately before the behavior and the general context at that time. Here you are looking for the common denominators. What evokes the behavior? What motivates it? Is the dog displaying typical fear-related behaviors during the incident? Get them all. If it is male strangers wearing hats, don't just write males or strangers. Be as specific as you can.

Note the consequences. What exactly follows each instance of the behavior? Chances are, the dog is escaping or avoiding something (some dogs just seem to love to fight, though, and this may involve some kind of physiological automatic positive reinforcement). What exactly is this dog getting out of this behavior? Note exactly what happens each time; this is probably what is driving the behavior. It is, at least, a good hypothesis for now.

Once you have taken your notes on what the behavior is, and what the antecedents and consequences have been in the past, and also have your paperwork on the ABCs after you have been tracking them for a little while, a somewhat clear picture should emerge regarding the antecedents and consequences and their relationship to the behaviors. In the table below, write the ABCs in.

| Antecedents | Behaviors | Consequences |
|---|---|---|
| | | |

Now it is time to put it all together. Write your contingency statement below. Make sure you describe, as concisely as possible, but also as specifically as possible, what the ABCs are in sentence form.

| Contingency Statement |
|---|
| |

# CHAPTER 5. BEHAVIOR CHANGE PROCEDURES AND CONSTRUCTING YOUR BEHAVIOR CHANGE PROGRAM

Now that we have a good idea of what the problem behavior is and why it occurs, we are in a position to make changes to the environment to change that behavior. The behavior change program is derived directly from the functional assessment. Unlike in the medical model approach, the assessment itself strongly suggests the approach to changing the behavior. Here I would like to start with outlining some options, then move to determining goals, then to basic principles and strategies, and then outline the most powerful behavior change procedures, based on respondent and operant principles. Finally, I deal with how to put it all together to come up with your plan of attack. I strongly recommend you work with a professional on this. This book is no replacement for the skill and judgment of a professional animal behavior consultant.

## Looking at Options

Generally, here are some of your options:

- euthanasia (kill the dog)
- rehome the dog
- micromanage the dog (prevention alone)
- behavior change program.

Killing the dog is an option, but I certainly hope not the one you choose. Under what circumstances might you be forced to consider this option? If the dog is extremely dangerous and has proven that by maiming or killing; if the stimulus that evokes the aggressive behavior cannot be avoided or predicted; if medical contributions have been ruled out to the best of your veterinarian's ability; and if there is no reasonable way to prevent the aggressive behavior, including through finding the dog a new home, then this option could be considered as a way to secure the safety of others. If this is not the case, though, I urge you to take responsibility for the problem. Your friend has some issues. It's not her "fault," and she is counting on you to help her resolve it.

Rehoming the dog is an option if the aggressive behavior is evoked by a stimulus that is present in your lifestyle and you cannot change it or cannot risk taking the chance of harm while you work on the problem, and this stimulus is not present in the lifestyle of someone who would be willing to take the dog, and these people know precisely what the problem behaviors are. For example, this sometimes occurs when the target is another household dog, or the family children. In a house with no other dogs or children, your dog might have a much better outlook. However, finding these homes is extremely difficult when people can just go to the shelter and adopt a dog who does not come with these risks. If you do find such a home, ensure in writing that the people adopting the dog understand the dog's history and the risks, and get a copy of that statement signed to protect you from liability.

In some cases, you can simply make changes to the environment that effectively minimize or remove the odds of the dog performing the behavior, even though there is no change to the contingencies involved. For example, let's say two dogs in the same house fight. Finding a home for the nonaggressive dog might be easy. In that case, you would keep the aggressive dog and simply never allow her access to other dogs. Or if a dog guards a toy, throw that toy away—if the behavior has generalized to all toys, you can try providing no toys at all. You have to be creative, and sometimes you do have to make sacrifices. It may mean no more walks in public or at least no more off-leash walks. It's not ideal, but you have to weigh the options. If you cannot proceed with a behavior change program for some reason, and you are able to use equipment or scheduling or otherwise arrange things to prevent evoking aggressive behaviors, then this option is one worth considering.

Constructing a behavior change program is the preferable choice, of course, because it not only minimizes the odds of the problem behavior occurring but also allows for a wider range of options for the dog. Instead of introducing a lot of restrictions, you can construct a program to change the behavior and work through it. This does not mean that you can let your guard down once you complete your protocols. You will have to remain vigilant in the future, but this option is best for everyone in most cases, and what this book is all about.

## Goals

Obviously, your goal is to put an end to the problem behavior. But it can help to give some thought to what will be realistic in your case and to set specific goals. Working with problem behavior takes time and work. Some behaviors are also more resistant to change than others. You might have a bare minimum goal that you must achieve in order to continue working on the problem. For example, if you have kids and the dog is aggressive toward them, you may have to set some tough goals to meet. If they are completely unrealistic (and a professional can help you determine what may or may not be realistic), then you should consider one of the other options. Be as generous as you can while taking into account what you can realistically expect to put into the problem. What follows is a discussion of some of the more important predictors of success. Consider these points when trying to decide on realistic goals.

If you are able to maintain control of the dog by preventing access to the stimuli that evoke the aggressive behavior, or through strong verbal control or the use of equipment, the likelihood of success will be greater than if you cannot manage the situation well.

If the dog is well trained, it will save much time and energy, and behavior change programs can be initiated sooner. If the dog is untrained, the task will be more challenging and time consuming.

The more biddable the dog is and the easier it is to identify high-value reinforcers for the dog, the easier will be the training. Adding desirable behavior to the dog's repertoire is an important part of many behavior change programs. If the dog is easily motivated, it will be much easier to adjust the environment to change the behavior. If the dog is socially motivated and finds human social contact a valuable reinforcer, this bodes well. Dogs who are aloof and independent may be more difficult to work with.

If there are young children or elderly, mobility-impaired or mentally impaired people in the house who might evoke the aggressive behavior, the risks will be greater than would otherwise be the case. These people are at risk largely because they are unlikely to be able to defend themselves or escape an attack.

The smaller the dog, the less risk is associated with their attacks and hence the more likely will be success. This is not to say that a hard bite from a toy-breed dog is not a painful experience. However, at about 40 pounds (18 kilograms), dogs become a much greater risk.

The harder the bite, the more dangerous is the situation. If the dog growls and snarls but does not bite, or if the bites only leave saliva, that is much better than if she actually punctures skin. It is even worse if damaging bites are deep or involve multiple bites or shaking while biting.

If you cannot afford a behavior consultant, veterinary tests, equipment and other necessary resources, you may be less likely to succeed. If you do not have the time to dedicate to training each day and for working on behavior change programs, then the likelihood of success is also lower. Changing behavior takes time.

If you are not committed to managing the dog's behavior in every situation, the risk is higher and the likelihood of success lower. You will need to be closely tuned in to your dog's behavior at every moment, and observant for potential problems. You must be able to handle tense situations and maintain this vigilance for the lifetime of the dog, as well as committing yourself to management and training for the dog's lifetime. Furthermore, everyone in the household should be committed. One person can sabotage a behavior change program if they are not on board.

Problems in which dogs who live together are fighting or one aggresses on another are really tough. It is difficult to keep the dogs separated, and often being separated contributes to the problem. Solutions are hard to find.

The more skilled your behavior consultant is, the greater the likelihood of success. If your behavior consultant is skilled at identifying the contingencies maintaining behavior, and at constructing behavior change programs that are efficient and within your ability to carry out, the likelihood of success is better than if the consultant is unskilled in these matters. The case will also progress better if the consultant is able to work flexibly with you and your needs than if the consultant is rigid and provides little or no support.

## Safety First

First things first. Before you construct a behavior change program, your first priority is to ensure that everyone will remain safe. Avoid allowing the dog to get herself into situations that may lead to aggression. This might require a bit of creativity. It might mean no walks or keeping two dogs separated. It might mean not allowing the dog into a particular room, or removing all toys, or not using a food dish at all. It might mean simply walking away rather than stepping over the dog or challenging her for a place on the couch. Ideally, prevent the whole context, but do not get into a challenge with the dog, as this will just entrench the problem further and will place you or others at risk. You will probably not be able to let the dog off leash outside of your house or yard.

A muzzle might be needed in certain situations where you cannot be sure aggressive displays will be prevented. Do not use the elastic-type "muzzles." They will not prevent bites. The material muzzles that keep the mouth closed are okay for brief periods when the weather is not hot and the dog will not be exercising or needing to drink. For other situations, and in fact in most situations, the basket-style muzzle is better. Never leave a dog unsupervised with a muzzle on. Introduce the muzzle gradually and pair it with treats and fun like walks or play. (Remember respondent conditioning of emotional responses—the aim is for the dog to have a positive emotional response to the muzzle.)

# Respondent-Conditioning-Based Behavior Change Procedures

Now that we understand the basics of respondent conditioning (see pages 34), let's describe the behavior change procedures that are based on it. Respondent-conditioning-based behavior change procedures are used to change emotional responses. There are more complicated concepts and more jargon coming, but don't worry too much about the words—just focus on getting a handle on how and why it works. Also, to prepare you ahead of time, I will be describing here the key behavior change procedures and strategies; later, I will describe how you will combine them in most cases.

## Counterconditioning

Counterconditioning, basically, involves countering respondent conditioning that has taken place; we counter problematic emotional responses with something incompatible with them. If your dog has developed a fear response to, say, people wearing hats, then we would counter that fear response with a joy response in its place. Or if your dog has developed an anxiety response to something (such as dogs with separation distress can develop to the routines their guardians use before leaving the house), then we would counter that anxiety with relaxation. We take a bad emotional response and replace it with a good emotional response. Remember that unpleasant emotional responses such as fear can motivate aggressive behaviors. The way to resolve these problem behaviors is to remove the motivation for them; if the dog learns to like people in hats (or other dogs, or the guardian picking up their keys in preparation to leave or whatever the case may be), then they have no reason to aggress and the problem is solved. Earlier I wrote that dogs do what works to get them what they want. Our goal with counterconditioning is to change what they want. Our goal with the operant approach (see below) will be to change what works.

Imagine that a person has come to fear snakes, but loves strawberry smoothies. Counterconditioning might involve presenting a snake, followed immediately by a sip of smoothie, and repeating this process until the presentation of the snake elicits a pleasant reaction instead of a fearful reaction. The order is important: the problem stimulus has to come just before the pleasurable stimulus. Likewise, if a dog is fearful of other dogs, but is delighted with little pieces of veggie burger, sessions could be arranged in which the dog is repeatedly presented with another dog, followed immediately by a piece of veggie burger, until the dog responds to other dogs with joy rather than fear. Don't get me wrong; it's not easy to change an emotional response, and it takes a lot of careful work.

Remember, in any instance where fear seems to be prominent, you need to identify the exact stimulus that elicits the fear. Don't define it too narrowly or too broadly. Look at what always leads to the fear response, find those common denominators, and that is your working hypothesis for the fear-eliciting stimulus. You also need to identify what the dog really loves too. What will elicit a joy response? Treats, games, social interaction? Keep in mind, it's not what *you* think the dog should find fun or tasty; be objective and find what *the dog* really will work for. To counter a strong emotional response, the thing that is used to counter it has to be exceptionally good.

Jean Donaldson (1998) coined the phrase "open bar—closed bar" to help describe this process, and described it well in her excellent book *Dogs are from Neptune*. When the fear-eliciting stimuli are presented, the bar is open, and treats (or games) flow freely and continuously. You should put a big smile on, tell the dog how good she is and dole out treats or play a game of tug. When the fear-eliciting stimulus goes away, the treat bar is closed, and life is a bit on the boring side. You may want to actually say something like "Woo hoo!" when the bar is open and "Bummer" when it closes so that the dog knows for sure when it starts and stops. The contrast helps enhance the conditioning. Opening the bar and closing the bar can be thought of as a hair-trigger light switch, turned on and off by the presence and absence of the fear-eliciting stimulus.

Ideally, there should be a 1:1 ratio between the presentation of fun stuff and the presentation of the fear-eliciting stimulus. That is, every time the fear-eliciting stimulus appears, so does the fun stuff. The effect will be weaker if one sometimes occurs without the other.

What if you are performing the procedure and the dog aggresses? We discussed this in Chapter 2 but I would like to reiterate it and elaborate on it here. First, of course, safety is of paramount consideration and we need to prepare our procedures accordingly, preventing the situation before it happens rather than responding once it does. You should be taking whatever precautions are necessary to ensure everyone's safety—muzzles where necessary, leashes attached to poles or eye-hooks in wall studs etc. But when a dog aggresses and your safety is accounted for, generally your best bet is to disengage from the situation early and without fuss. Stop presenting the feared stimulus, either by removing it or the dog from the environment. It is true that this might reinforce the behavior, because the dog learns that the aggressive behavior "works" to allow her to escape from the situation. However, putting an end to the aggressive display early rather than allowing it to continue prevents escalation of the behavior and reinforcement of that escalated behavior, and reduces the stress and aversive quality of the event for the dog. It's not ideal, and you should aim to avoid allowing the dog to aggress or become fearful, but if you make a mistake, push too far and she does aggress, put a stop to the session. Recognize this as a mistake and a setback. If the dog is on leash and the target is not you, walk away with her. If you are the target or the dog is stationary, then move yourself or the target away from the dog immediately. End the session and don't perform it again that day; when a dog aggresses or becomes fearful, her brain chemistry is all out of whack and it will take quite some time to normalize (and during that time she will be primed to aggress further). Remember too: intense fear and aggressive behavior are the antithesis of counterconditioning. The whole premise on which counterconditioning is based is that joy or relaxation is elicited and intense fear is not. A fear response is a step back, so prevent it where possible. If you accidentally allow the dog to become intensely fearful, nothing further beneficial can be achieved in that session. In that case, end the session without further fuss and try again, more carefully, the next day.

The only other way to avoid reinforcing aggressive behaviors is to wait through the aggressive display until you get nonaggressive behaviors. You can then reinforce these acceptable behaviors with treats or by removing the dog from the situation at that point. There are some risks with this strategy, however. One is that you may actually train the dog to aggress so that she can then stop aggressing in order to get the treats (something we call a behavior chain). The other is that keeping the dog in the situation might be dangerous and certainly will be unpleasant for the dog.

In short, the safest option is to remove the dog and yourself quickly and early so as not to encourage more intense aggressive behaviors. It is the lesser of evils. Ideally, the goal is to proactively prevent the aggressive display altogether through graded and incremental approaches to training. If aggressive behavior is occurring frequently, then you need to tighten up control of the environment. The goal is to work through the training at a level that keeps the dog below her threshold for showing aggressive responses so that beneficial learning takes place. There is a way to make this process work, and that is what we turn to now.

## Systematic Desensitization

The problem with counterconditioning on its own is that if we simply present the fear- or anxiety-eliciting stimulus and the treats and games, the fear and anxiety may be so strong that the emotional response does not change; the treats and games may just get overshadowed by the emotional response. Systematic desensitization is the answer. Systematic desensitization is counterconditioning carried out in a graded, stepwise (incremental) manner that helps ensure that the process does not get overshadowed by strong emotional responses. Systematic desensitization procedures consist of three components:

- promoting or maintaining relaxation
- constructing a stimulus exposure hierarchy
- counterconditioning.

Promoting relaxation in dogs can mean using massage or TTouch™, or moderate exercise. Regular routine and lack of frustration or aversive stimulation can help ensure that the dog is as relaxed as possible for the desensitization procedure. It definitely means trying to avoid things that the dog finds stressful prior to performing the procedure, and choosing times when the dog is already relaxed. The important thing is to go into each session with the dog as relaxed as possible.

The next component is the construction of a stimulus exposure hierarchy. This is a list, in rank order, of stimuli that cause problems for the dog, from least problematic to most problematic. In constructing the stimulus exposure hierarchy, the aim should be to start with a level that elicits the dog's attention but not fear. The gap between levels should be small in order to avoid a strong emotional response in the dog. Problem stimuli may involve many variables or dimensions, and it is usually a good idea to identify the variables that can be separated and work with them separately. Some common variables are:

- distance (between the dog and the feared stimulus)
- duration (for which the stimulus is present)
- distraction (by other things going on in the environment)
- orientation (for example, of the feared person or dog to the subject dog)

- sudden contrast (such as remaining still and quiet versus making quick movements or noise).

Each dog is a unique individual, as is each problem emotional response. Let us assume, for example, that a dog is fearful of strangers. At 20 feet, the dog orients and attends to the stranger; at 15 feet, she stiffens and stares; and at 12 feet, she snarls. If the person is facing her and approaching, she will lunge at 10 feet, biting if she can, whereas, if the stranger is facing away and remaining still, she will lunge at 7 feet, and snap and bite when the stranger is within striking distance at, say, 2 feet. This information allows for construction of a stimulus exposure hierarchy. The most prominent variable in this case (as is usually the case) is distance. The degree of "strangeness" or novelty, orientation and sudden contrast are also important. In some cases, variables can be clumped together, as in the example below.

Once the stimulus exposure hierarchy has been constructed, the next step is to work through the hierarchy, with counterconditioning taking place at each step. Here is what this program might look like:

- Levels 1–10: Semi-stranger (whom the dog has seen on previous occasions), oriented away and making no sudden movements or loud noises.

1. Approach to 20 feet.
2. Approach to 18 feet.
3. Approach to 15 feet.
4. Approach to 12 feet.
5. Approach to 10 feet.
6. Approach to 8 feet.
7. Approach to 6 feet.
8. Approach to 5 feet.
9. Approach to 4 feet.
10. Approach to 3 feet.

Once this hierarchy is complete, move on to the next one:

- Levels 11–20: Same as last hierarchy, but the person is oriented towards the dog.

Once this hierarchy is complete, move on to the next one:

- Levels 21–32: Same as last hierarchy, but the person is oriented towards the dog and speaking to the guardian in a friendly tone, and the final approach is closer.

  21. Approach to 20 feet.
  22. Approach to 18 feet.
  23. Approach to 15 feet.
  24. Approach to 12 feet.
  25. Approach to 10 feet.
  26. Approach to 8 feet.
  27. Approach to 6 feet.
  28. Approach to 5 feet.
  29. Approach to 4 feet.
  30. Approach to 3 feet.
  31. Approach to 2 feet.
  32. Approach to 1 foot. The dog will probably sniff/investigate the stranger.

Once this hierarchy is complete, move on to the next one:

- Levels 33–44: Same as last hierarchy, but the person briefly looks softly at the dog. Duration of soft look is increased through subsequent steps.

Once this hierarchy is complete, move on to the next one:

- Levels 45–90: Repeat the entire process, this time with a real stranger.

Once this hierarchy is complete, move on to the next one:

- Levels 91–180: Repeat the entire process with yet another stranger to help generalize the response. Carry it out in different locations. Once the hierarchy has been run a couple of times, it will become smoother and easier to work through successive hierarchies.

The hierarchy can, of course, be fine-tuned for your particular goals. If you would like the dog to accept petting or handling of some specific kind, you should now incorporate that, running the exercises of the hierarchy while relaxing other variables.

Constructing stimulus exposure hierarchies is a skill, requiring creativity, experience and good judgment. Also important is a thorough familiarity with the dog, the problem stimuli and the dog's thresholds for different types of aggressive behaviors at different intensities of exposure to the problem stimuli.

The sample hierarchy above could easily have been constructed differently, clumping different variables together and splitting others, or running some sequences in a different order. You should remain flexible. For example, it may be necessary to break a step into a few smaller steps because the dog is tensing up when a change is made. The goal is to get through the process with as few aggressive reactions as possible (none, ideally) and incorporate what could be expected of the dog in real life. You must carefully observe the dog so that you can stop the exercise at the very first sign that the dog's arousal level is increasing. If this happens, it should be considered a setback because there is a risk that the behaviors associated with arousal could be reinforced. In this situation, you should learn from the mistake and move more slowly at each level next time or choose smaller steps.

Be prepared—systematic desensitization is often slow, painstaking work with frequent setbacks. If you expect this, you will be more likely to get through it successfully.

It is important to remember that what we believe is relaxing or enjoyable and what is actually relaxing or enjoyable to the dog may be two different things. Always observe the dog's behavior for guidance on what is relaxing or enjoyable. Relaxation is particularly helpful when desensitizing to anxiety-eliciting stimuli. Remember that we always need to go into these sessions with a relaxed dog. If the problem is anxiety (for example, separation anxiety), then we usually just countercondition the anxiety with relaxation. For fear-eliciting stimuli, which are common in aggression cases, something that elicits pleasure is also helpful. This can include favored treats, verbal praise, social contact and play. So, at each level you are working during a session, remember to pair the problem stimulus with something pleasant. Once you get to a point where the dog sees the problem stimulus and immediately looks eager or pleased, you know she is making the association: the stranger = treats or fun and games. That's excellent, and means you are ready to go on to the next level in the hierarchy to repeat the process.

# Operant-Conditioning-Based Behavior Change Procedures

Procedures based on operant conditioning are used to change voluntary, goal-directed behaviors. Below we will explore the most powerful and useful of these procedures.

## Behavior Replacement

### *The Strategy*

There are two basic philosophies about how to go about changing operant behavior. In the past, the "eliminative approach" was popular. This involves punishing undesirable behaviors to eliminate them. After all, punishment decreases the frequency of behavior and that is what we want, right? Right, but using aversive techniques leads to some insidious behavioral side effects (see page 85) and also raises serious ethical questions. The "constructional approach" replaced this old approach. The constructional approach seeks to increase, rather than decrease, the dog's repertoire of behaviors. It is ingenious, actually. Instead of punishing undesirable behaviors to eliminate them, we replace the problem behavior with a desirable behavior. The dog is obviously seeking a reinforcer of some kind and she is choosing which behaviors to use to get it. By punishing the behavior, we not only expose the dog to an unpleasant experience, which leads to problems, but we usually fail to address the sought-after reinforcement. In the constructional approach, we make use of that reinforcer or, if that's undesirable for some reason, we make use of other, high-value reinforcers, to reinforce a different behavior instead. If we manipulate the environment to make some other behavior more worthwhile, then we effectively control the behavior. And that is exactly what we are going to do—we'll replace the aggressive behavior with something else and make that pay off big time for the dog.

We need to add another component to this process, though. We have to arrange it so that the choice to perform aggressive behaviors is as unlikely as possible and the choice to perform some other behavior is more likely. But we don't achieve that by punishing aggressive behaviors. We achieve it by installing the new behavior in such small steps that the dog has a chance to learn the new contingency (antecedent, behavior and reinforcer) the easy way. These small steps are constructed in a similar way to the process we used for systematic desensitization.

So, the goal will be to start out on the edge of the dog's comfort zone, close enough to the problem stimulus that she attends to it but doesn't become fearful, and we reinforce a more desirable behavior. We make this reinforcer highly valuable. Because the problem stimulus is not at full intensity, the dog is unlikely to choose aggressive behaviors.

The first task is to identify the undesirable behavior you wish to replace. If it is a single behavior, write that down. If it is a sequence of behaviors that occur together, you can write them all down together. It must be a discrete, observable behavior (or list of behaviors if they always occur together), not a label (e.g., dominance aggression, or territorial aggression or the like) and not an interpretation (e.g., spite, crazy behavior, flipping out). This is the behavior or behavior set that we need to avoid by keeping the dog below her threshold (subthreshold) for aggressive behavior.

The next task is to identify the replacement behavior. You have some basic choices here. You can choose between these options:

- other behavior
- incompatible behavior
- alternative behavior.

When we target an "other" behavior for positive reinforcement, we set the rule that we will reinforce any behavior at all other than the problem behavior we have identified. If you decide to use this procedure, you prevent the target aggressive behaviors, and you offer positive reinforcement for anything else that the dog does. The upside of this option is that, if you are reinforcing calm, relaxed (nonaggressive and nonfearful) behaviors, then you may be reinforcing behaviors that influence the underlying "mood." The downside of this option is that you are not installing a specific behavior, and so the choice may not always be as clear for the dog what *else* to do.

When we target an "incompatible" behavior for positive reinforcement, we set the rule that we will reinforce a specific behavior that is mutually exclusive to the problem behavior. For example, the dog cannot be lunging and biting passersby if she is sitting and watching you. The upside of this approach is that you target a specific behavior and if the dog chooses to perform it then there is no way she can also be aggressing. You can train this specific behavior outside of the problem situation to a good level of reliability and then apply it to the problem situation. The downside of this approach is that you cannot always identify an incompatible behavior that is also a viable option in a given situation.

69

When we target an "alternative" behavior for positive reinforcement, we set the rule that we will reinforce a specific behavior other than the problem behavior, but it is not necessarily incompatible with the problem behavior. It is not always easy to identify an incompatible behavior, and in these instances, reinforcing merely an alternative specific behavior is a good choice. Again, you can train this behavior beforehand and apply it to the problem situation once it is good and solid.

In choosing replacement behaviors, the behavior selected should allow the dog to access natural, everyday reinforcement in the long run (as opposed to contrived reinforcers like treats). One option is to reinforce nonaggressive investigation of the problem stimulus (looking at it nonaggressively, sniffing, approaching etc.). Another option is to reinforce an incompatible behavior, such as looking away from and/or walking away from the problem stimulus and to the handler instead. The choice of behavior will depend on the individual dog and the context of the problem behavior. You should write down the steps and criteria for the chosen procedure so that everyone working with the dog can stay clear on the goals and procedures. Your consultant should demonstrate the techniques and have you perform them under their supervision, at least until they are sure you understand the process.

The incremental, graded approach is all about preventing the dog from becoming fearful or aggressive. If the dog becomes fearful or aggressive, her emotional response will interfere with learning. So, the goal when training the dog to perform the replacement behavior is to start at a distance that does not elicit fear or evoke aggressive displays; only when you have the behavior good and solid at that low intensity do you increase the intensity a small amount and do it again. You arrange the sessions in a graded, incremental fashion so that the dog is not pushed past her threshold for aggressing but is still aware of the stimulus that usually evokes it, and this gives you the chance to get and reinforce your replacement behavior.

Just as we devised a hierarchy of intensity in systematic desensitization, we do the same thing now, while installing the replacement behavior. For example, if the dog attends to approaching strangers at 25 feet, stares and stiffens up when strangers approach to 20 feet, growls when they get to 15 feet, snarls and lunges when they get to 10 feet and snaps or bites when they get to 5 feet, then you know that you have a better chance of getting your replacement behavior instead of aggressive behaviors if you maintain the stranger at 25 feet. Does this remind you of systematic desensitization? It should, because both involve a gradual, incremental approach that keeps the dog "subthreshold," just on the edge of her comfort zone. This gives us the opportunity to teach her a better way to handle her stress without aggressing, and we cannot do that if she is lunging and snapping. In this example, you would make an arrangement with a "stranger" to approach to 25 feet (perhaps marked with tape), and you get and reinforce your target behavior. Repeat that many times and you'll find it gets easier and easier. In fact, you should start to see that the dog performs the behavior as soon as she sees the stimulus in question rather than waiting for your cue (the stranger becomes the antecedent rather than your verbal cue). When that is going well and the dog performs the behavior automatically when she sees the stranger at that distance, then you know you are probably ready to take it to, say, 21 feet. Repeat the process, getting closer each time.

The beauty of carrying out these sessions, maintaining the dog subthreshold but still attending to the stimulus, is that the dog does not aggress, you avoid the side effects of having to perform aversive procedures, you avoid the risk of reinforcing aggressive behaviors, and you get the job done. The dog learns that, if she performs this replacement behavior when she sees the "stranger," it will pay off. Because we did not push it to what seems to the dog to threaten her survival, she is more likely to perform that behavior. Wonderful! This gradual, incremental approach allows us to train the dog to perform the desired behavior in the presence of the problem stimulus rather than choosing the aggressive option; we give the dog a chance to learn that she can, in fact, make another choice and that the other choice will pay off!

There is something else going on when we arrange it this way (which I will elaborate on below under "Putting it All Together" on page 90). Remember I pointed out that operant and respondent conditioning are always taking place, at the same time? Well, by taking this graded, incremental approach, you are not only installing a desirable replacement behavior; you are also counterconditioning the emotional response. (At the same time, another learning process called habituation is probably also occurring—the dog gets used to the problem stimulus just by being around it so much.) Think about it; while you are preventing aggressive displays and training the dog to perform a desirable, voluntary behavior with positive reinforcement, you are also presenting the provocative stimulus at an intensity that does not encourage the dog to react aggressively and presenting pleasurable stimuli (treats or a game or whatever you use). The provocative stimulus is now going to start eliciting joy rather than fear; she will see the "stranger" and think "Yippy, treats are coming, strangers rock!" That is the genius of this approach. You can achieve the goal of changing both the voluntary aggressive behaviors and the emotional responses that motivate them at the same time.

In any behavior replacement procedure, then, you start by identifying both a specific behavior or set of behaviors to prevent (by manipulating distance, orientation, distraction level etc.) and a replacement behavior for positive reinforcement. You can train the replacement behavior outside of the problem context first and then, once it is good and solid in a wide variety of contexts, you can start introducing it to the problem situation. You identify a high-value reinforcer you can use and a behavior that suits your goals and is easy for the dog to perform (one that seems natural in the situation, if possible). Then you write up the hierarchy of exposure to the problem stimulus as it stands now, taking into account the variables important to the intensity of exposure (as with constructing the hierarchy for systematic desensitization). Write it out in steps. Then it is a matter of carrying out the plan. Present the stimulus at a level just intense enough to arouse attention but not enough to evoke aggressive behaviors. Get the replacement behavior and reinforce it. Make it all very fun. Repeat, working your way gradually through the hierarchy.

Below, I would like to elaborate on manipulating antecedents so that you can go in with the best odds possible for getting the desirable behavior and not the aggressive behaviors.

### Manipulating Antecedents (Antecedent Control Procedures)

We can do more to encourage the desirable behavior and discourage the undesirable behavior than merely making the provocative stimulus evoke a replacement behavior in place of an aggressive behavior. Remember, to change behavior we change the environment that sustains it. That means making changes to the A (antecedents—things that come before the behavior), as well as the C (consequences—things that come after the behavior). Although most people are focused on the consequences, adjusting the antecedents can really improve your odds. Antecedent control is a term used to describe the measures we can take to address what comes before the behavior.

There are three types of antecedents:

- setting events
- motivating operations
- discriminative stimuli.

You won't have to remember all of these categories. Just give thought to your own case as you read about them and take notes on how they might apply to what you are working on. What they all have in common is that they are things that make a behavior more or less likely. That is important because our goal is to make desirable replacement behaviors more likely and aggressive behaviors less likely. Making the aggressive behaviors less likely and the replacement behavior more likely will go a long way to ensuring the success of your behavior change program, and you can use all the help you can get; attack the problem on as many fronts as possible. I will describe each type of antecedent briefly so that you can think about how you can apply these principles and strategies to the problem you face.

**Setting events** are the general circumstances surrounding the behavior. They may not immediately evoke the behavior, but nevertheless, they have some influence over it. You may find that the time of day may be relevant—for example, that your dog only aggresses in the morning, even though she faces the same problem stimuli distributed throughout the day (this may also mean you simply have not nailed down what exactly *is* evoking the behavior). Pay attention to the general circumstances that may influence whether the dog performs the behavior or not.

**Motivating operations** relate to how motivated the dog is to perform either the desirable or the undesirable behavior; this term specifically relates to how valuable the reinforcer involved is. If you are using treats and the dog is full of dinner, then the treats will not work as well as a motivator or reinforcer. If you are using a toy and the dog has already been playing with it all morning, then it is unlikely to be very valuable. Emotional responses contribute to motivation, too. If a dog is afraid of something, she will be motivated to perform behaviors that allow her to escape or avoid it—escape or avoidance will be a higher value reinforcer than it would be otherwise. If she enjoys something, she will be motivated to perform behaviors that help her access that thing. In terms of the ABCs of behavior, the C reinforces the voluntary behaviors involved. The stimuli that come before the behavior (the A) elicit the emotions that then make that reinforcer more valuable. These stimuli both provoke the emotional response (usually fear) and indicate to the dog that aggressive behaviors will pay off (enabling the dog to avoid or escape the stimuli). See how it all fits together? In the framework of the ABCs, emotional responses play into the A that motivates the B. The important thing to remember here is that emotional responses motivate behaviors because they make certain reinforcers more or less valuable. If we are clever, we can arrange this in our favor.

**Discriminative stimulus** is a fancy term for the stimulus that evokes the behavior, occurring immediately before it. Many trainers use the term "trigger" to describe this stimulus (although this is not ideal since it seems to imply that the stimulus automatically causes the behavior, whereas it is more a matter of probability). The discriminative stimulus (or evoking stimulus, if you prefer) says to the dog that behavior X will pay off in this situation. Our goal is to make the stimulus evoke the desirable behavior rather than the undesirable behavior. As we discussed above, we do that by repeatedly making the desirable behavior pay off and the undesirable behavior unlikely.

**Response effort** is something else you should consider. It refers to how much effort is required to perform a behavior. Ensure that the replacement behavior you choose is easy to perform; that is, it should be a natural behavior in the situation. If possible, make the undesirable behavior require more effort and the desirable behavior require less effort. It's more difficult (and near impossible) to lunge at strangers if you are on a leash, for example. Looking at your handler as you pass strangers is fairly easy and is often a good choice.

The take-home message here is: don't just consider and change the consequences; also consider what comes before the behavior—what motivates it, provokes it and generally makes the behavior more or less likely to occur, and address these things too. Things like nutrition, exercise, mental stimulation and even the effect of medications or supplements on the physiology of the dog are all part of the context in which behaviors are more or less likely. This systematic approach attacks the problem on all fronts.

### Some Common Antecedent Control Procedures

Adjusting the antecedents to a behavior can mean changing setting events, motivating operations or discriminative stimuli. Common procedures for addressing setting events are described later in this section.

With regard to motivating operations, make sure the dog does not always have access to the reinforcers you want to use to make your replacement behavior a better choice. If you use a toy, keep it out of sight most of the time. If you use treats, pick the best treats and use them primarily for these exercises. Addressing what comes before a behavior should also include addressing the emotional responses that motivate aggressive behaviors (emotional motivating operations). Systematic desensitization or a behavior replacement program that also helps change emotional responses is helpful in this regard.

The discriminative stimulus, as we discussed, is the immediate antecedent to the behavior. It is the thing that comes right before the behavior. For example, it can be other dogs, strangers, or people approaching the dog when she eats. This will be the stimulus we will design the behavior change program around. If you set up a systematic desensitization program or a behavior replacement program, then you'll design a hierarchy of exposure leading to full intensity encounters with that stimulus.

When designing a behavior change program, you should try to make use of as many of the strategies described here as possible (the shotgun approach). Antecedent control procedures are particularly useful when used for both desirable and undesirable behaviors, in conjunction with one another. For instance, a dog will be encouraged to choose a desirable behavior over an undesirable behavior if the discriminative stimulus for the undesirable behavior is removed while the discriminative stimulus for the desirable behavior is simultaneously presented, and if it is also easier for the dog to access the reinforcer using the desirable behavior, and if the value of the reinforcer is also increased through motivating operations. Dogs always have a choice as to which behavior they will perform. Some are more strongly motivated, so that it is not apparent that there is a choice, but that simply means that the dog's decision is obvious; one option efficiently achieves a far higher value reinforcer, and this is the one that will be chosen. By manipulating the antecedents, we can arrange the economics of the situation such that the dog will be more likely to choose the desirable behavior. If you can get into the habit of thinking of behavior as always involving a choice among alternatives, you will be more likely to be thinking about how you can make a desirable behavior a better choice than the undesirable behavior. This, as part of a behavior replacement procedure, is a systematic and powerful strategy for changing the behavior of animals. Applying antecedent control procedures is a very creative process, requiring knowledge, experience and, sometimes, some lateral thinking skills.

The following points are relevant to the decision about which, if any, antecedent control procedures to implement:

- What conditions (e.g., specific places or times) are the problem behaviors correlated with? Can we prevent access to those conditions?
- What are the reinforcers involved in the desirable and undesirable behaviors? Can we make the appropriate reinforcers more or less valuable, respectively?
- What are the discriminative stimuli controlling the desirable and undesirable behaviors? Can we make it so that the discriminative stimulus for the undesirable behavior is removed, either completely or partially? Can we make it so that the discriminative stimulus for the desirable behavior is present in more (or all) of the appropriate

situations? Can we make the discriminative stimulus for the desirable behavior more prominent?

- What effort is required for the desirable and undesirable behavior? Can we make it a bit more difficult to perform the undesirable behavior and easier to perform the desirable behavior? Can we choose a desirable behavior that is easier to perform?

Now, let's turn to describing a few standard antecedent control procedures (the more distant ones—setting events) that are commonly helpful in changing the environment (both within and outside of the body) that sets the occasion for aggressive behaviors.

Remember that aggressive behavior is set in the context of the whole animal. The physiology of the dog is part of the "environment" in a way, because it contributes to the behavior. It is beyond the scope of this book to get too deeply into the physiology of aggressive behavior, but suffice it to say that we can promote physiological states that are beneficial or detrimental to the dog's behavior. One goal is to promote serotonin activity within the dog's brain. Serotonin is the feel-good neurotransmitter (a neurotransmitter is a chemical that communicates between cells in the brain). Exercise and diet can help promote more serotonin activity.

### Training

Verbal control of any dog who makes use of aggressive behaviors is important. Verbal control will not only give you a way to prevent or interrupt problem behaviors, but will also allow the opportunity to install replacement behaviors more easily. A well-trained dog is also more likely to take direction, which can influence the probability of aggressive behavior.

Another benefit to training in general, as long as the process remains fun and the contingencies are clear, is that the dog becomes empowered. Dogs learn that they can make effective choices in their lives, and this ability creates confidence and resilience. Training in this way can be particularly useful for dogs who may have learned that their environment operates outside of their control. For dogs with various levels of learned helplessness, training in a fun way promotes empowerment and can be rehabilitating.

Group classes may be out of the question if your dog is aggressive, but you may be able to find a trainer to work one on one with you, or your behavior consultant might work with you on the basics. If you'll be working through this on your own, I suggest working with a good book. *The Culture Clash* by Jean Donaldson is an excellent book, which will provide you not only with excellent training advice but with much more on dog behavior in general. *Getting Started: Clicker Training for Dogs* by Karen Pryor is another good book, smaller and mainly on training the basics. *The Power of Positive Dog Training* by Pat Miller is another excellent choice.

### *Play*

Play leads to emotional responses that are incompatible with aggression; it counterconditions fear or anxiety responses. Play can be used to promote a less hostile environment, thereby reducing the probability of aggressive behaviors. Furthermore, it can build confidence, improve behavioral flexibility and empowerment, and improve the relationship between you and the dog by increasing the positive reinforcements in both your lives and mending strained relationships. Play is also a major source of bonding between dogs. Through play, dogs learn how to relate socially to others in a nonhostile context. Research shows that play can result in increased confidence.

Play should be constructive and structured, and play sessions can be used as reinforcement for training. If the dog loves her throw-toy or a tug-toy, a brief toss or tug can be used as reinforcement during training sessions. Tug-of-war can be a particularly useful game. It can also help in training the dog to take and release items on cue. And, of course, it can be fun, which is beneficial to the human–dog relationship. Another useful thing about tug-of-war is that it can be done quickly, in small bouts, while the dog remains on leash (in contrast to fetch, for example). Tug-of-war (and indeed fetch) can be helpful adjuncts to changing the behavior of dogs who guard resources (such as food and toys), by making cooperative handling of the guarded item reinforcing, provided that these games are introduced carefully. The rules for tug-of-war must be maintained consistently. They are:

- Any contact of tooth to skin immediately results in the end of the game and no access to reinforcement for a few moments.
- You, not the dog, initiate the game always (to discourage the dog from initiating tug-of-war games at dangerous or otherwise inappropriate times).
- The dog takes her end of the tug toy, only on cue.
- The dog releases the toy when cued to do so.

Tug-of-war is not appropriate in all cases, obviously. If the dog is not careful and bites, or becomes too aroused during this kind of play and aggresses, then this kind of play is out.

Fetch is another excellent form of play. Some dogs take quickly and naturally to it, and others can learn it with a bit of training. Sometimes extensive training is required for the dog to learn fetch. If training is needed, it might not be as intrinsically fun for the dog, and other forms of play could be explored.

In some situations, dogs must be prepared before play can be used. Some dogs respond aggressively to any form of social control or have simply not learned to find play reinforcing, and some dogs are extremely independent, finding little reinforcement in social contact with people. Use of play with such dogs is inappropriate, at least at first, and can be dangerous. In these situations, play activities must be introduced carefully, slowly and on the dog's schedule. This might involve building on a dog's minor play attempts or solicitations, encouraging the dog to engage playfully and allowing her to experience play as a reinforcing event.

Many people use play that they, rather than the dog, find fun, or they misinterpret what the dog finds enjoyable. Observe the dog's behavior carefully and identify explicitly what the dog finds fun and not so fun, distinct from your own expectations or assumptions.

### Exercise

"A tired dog is a good dog." There seems to be a physiological basis for this adage. Research indicates that aerobic, predictable and rhythmical exercise of moderate to high intensity is likely to be helpful in several ways. It can provide a stress-buffering effect, stave off learned helplessness, improve cognitive function, result in less emotionality and encourage greater confidence. The relationship and communication between you and your dog are also likely to improve if you participate in exercise together, and this may improve your commitment to other interventions. Individual exercise sessions may have some benefits, but more stable results may be seen after 6 weeks of moderate to intense exercise sessions, 5 days per week, for at least 1 hour each session. This is only a general recommendation. Dogs must be conditioned gradually for this kind of exercise, and breeds will vary (often drastically) in what they can handle and what they require. Some terrier breeds, for example, may require more intense exercise rather than moderate exercise.

The first step in designing an exercise program is to assess the dog. The dog should undergo a full veterinary evaluation to identify any structural or other medical issues that might affect how she should be exercised. Ensure you include warm-ups and cool-downs in each exercise session. Dogs under 18 months of age require large amounts of exercise, but should avoid any form of exercise that is jarring on the joints, especially for large-breed dogs. Certain breeds, such as Siberian Huskies and Border Collies, were bred to require extreme amounts of physical exercise. Generally, sled dogs, herding dogs and sporting dogs require hours of exercise each day. Certain sight hounds, such as the Greyhound, are not very active generally but have spurts of energy, during which they will run around as fast as they can. It can be difficult to convince some breeds such as the English Bulldog to exercise; given the chance, they would choose to lie on the couch. Speaking of the Bulldog, it is important to note that brachycephalic (short-muzzled) dogs can have trouble breathing when they exert themselves. It is especially important to be careful when introducing physical exercise in these breeds.

The three main variables in an exercise program are intensity, duration and frequency. The goal will depend on the breed and particular dog, but a general rule might be for a moderate to intense session of 1–1.5 hours per day, four or five times per week. Some general principles to keep in mind are as follows:

- The duration of exercise should be inversely proportional to the intensity. That is, if the dog is working very hard, the session should be short.

- During intense exercise sessions, take frequent play and rest breaks. Rest breaks should be similar to cool-downs, rather than being sudden stops.

- Cross-training is an excellent way to keep the dog in the game and condition different muscle groups. Swimming and fetch or jogging is a great combination. This helps prevent wear and tear on specific structures due to repetitive movements.

- Always watch for signs of fatigue and use changes in intensity and rest breaks to manage them. A dog who is fatigued frequently may begin to dislike exercise. Look for:

  - lying down (often in the middle of a task) or remaining down when encouraged to do something
  - excess panting (perhaps with widening at the end of the tongue)

- yawning
- general lack of enthusiasm or energy
- stumbling
- anxiety, indicated by stressed facial expression (wide grin with furrows under eyes behind the mouth)
- dragging feet when trotting (often you hear the nails scraping on the ground).

- Vary the intensity, duration and, to a lesser extent, the frequency of exercise to keep it stimulating. These aspects should be varied in an apparently random manner, but the averages should continue to increase gradually during conditioning. Once initial conditioning is complete, intensity, duration and frequency should stay about the same, but perhaps one day could be moderate intensity for a longer duration and the next day a shorter but more intense session could be used. Amounts of exercise should not vary drastically but just enough to keep it exciting and prevent staleness.

- Try to vary the tasks and exercises within individual sessions in order to help maintain enthusiasm and prevent staleness or injury.

- Provide some water before, during and after exercise, but avoid allowing the dog to gulp large quantities at once.

- Avoid exercising in very hot temperatures. On a hot day, reduce the intensity and duration of exercise and observe the dog carefully for signs of fatigue. Take frequent rest breaks and try to be out of direct sunlight.

Exercise can be overdone. In North America, it is common for dogs to be under-exercised, but in some parts of Europe, it is common for many dogs to be over-exercised. Adequate and effective exercise is a balance; avoid under- or over-doing it.

The type of exercise done should reflect the dog's structure, conditioning and even evolutionary history. Some dogs will fetch till the cows come home, for example, and so fetch can often be a great way to get rolling with an exercise program. Other dogs do not fetch; although they can be trained to do so, another preference—such as jogging or swimming—might be a better choice. To produce calming effects and other benefits relating to aggression problems, the exercise should be aerobic, rhythmic and predictable.

The type of exercise chosen should relate not only to the dog's particular structure, physical condition and predilections but also what will be acceptable to you. For some, swimming is not possible due to lack of facilities, and others may find running with the dog impossible. Here are some ideas:

- Mechanical treadmills are great and allow for exercise inside when weather is bad. Unfortunately, they are expensive, take up a lot of space and may become boring to some dogs.

- Trotting is great and is acceptable for most dogs, although it may be difficult for many people to jog for long enough to provide sufficient exercise for the dog. Playing fetch during the walk can increase the dog's exercise on each walk.

- Trotting alongside a bicycle or inline skates allows you to keep up with the dog more easily but can be risky with most dogs. In most cases, the risks outweigh the benefits.

- Fetch is a great way to allow the dog to exercise while you remain stationary. Items to fetch include balls, Kongs™ on ropes—which allow you to throw the toy further—and ChuckIts™, a plastic arm that grabs a tennis ball and allows the ball to be thrown greater distances. For golfers, Hyper Doggie Drivers can be used to drive tennis balls large distances. For some dogs, fetch may be too intense an exercise. Longer duration, moderate exercise is beneficial, but intense, short bursts of exercise may cause stress.

- Swimming is one of the very best exercises because it has low impact on the joints but provides the same benefits as other aerobic exercise programs. Where the facilities exist, it can be a fun and acceptable form of exercise. Swimming can be encouraged by using a fetch toy—such as a Cool Kong™ or red fetch dummy device (usually good for natural bodies of water)—or by attaching a harness and leash to encourage swimming around the edge of pools. Swimming is particularly reinforcing for dogs that were bred to perform in water. Many retrievers are well suited to water exercise. However, some dogs are fearful of water and may have to be gently accustomed to it. Some breeds with deep chests (such as Boxers) tend to sink and can have real trouble swimming easily. Personal flotation devices can be used where necessary.

- Some dogs, such as Huskies and Malamutes, love the snow and love to pull. Mushing or skijoring (in which the dog pulls a person on skis) can be a great way for these dogs to get exercise. Many of these Nordic breeds respond best to moderately intense, long-duration exercise sessions like these. Obviously, many breeds, particularly the ones that do not tolerate cold well (such as Greyhounds), will not respond well to these ideas, and some dogs are too small.

- Agility can be a wonderful way to get exercise. It promotes cooperation between you and the dog and provides good exercise for both team members. Unfortunately, most aggressive dogs should not be allowed off leash in public, but it may be possible under some circumstances.

- Flyball can be good exercise for some dogs, as long as it is not risky to allow them off leash. Flyball usually involves high-intensity exercise, and warm-ups and cool-downs are imperative. This option would be best for breeds that are most suited to very intense exercise, such as some terriers.

- Dog–dog play can be excellent exercise for dogs who do not pose a risk to other dogs. For aggressive dogs, it may not be possible to visit the local dog park, but another option is to arrange meetings between certain playmates under controlled circumstances. Some dogs (particularly young dogs) will exercise intensely playing with other dogs, and they will usually manage their own intensity and duration of exercise. The motivation to continue playing is usually quite easy and natural. Dog–dog social play also provides a very fun experience, incompatible with aggression (unless arousal is a problem).

- Play between dogs and humans can be fun and provide excellent exercise, if it can be performed safely. Play can also be a good way to reinforce other less reinforcing forms of exercise. Of course, it is vitally important that the play not provoke the dog to behave aggressively or pose a risk to anyone. Some dogs like to be chased, and others like to chase. Some dogs like to play tug-of-war, while others prefer mock combat. I have seen no evidence that any of these activities contributes to aggressive behavior generally. Rules of social play need to be maintained: you should initiate and terminate all play and should be able to stop play on cue; the dog should never (even accidentally) bite anyone; if tug-of-war is the game, the dog should take the tug-toy and drop it on cue.

### Nutritional Support

You are what you eat. There is some support for manipulation of diet to change behavior. I recommend a diet that is moderate in protein content (approximately 18% as fed at 10% moisture) and does not contain corn. Vegetarian diets usually have a relatively low protein content and higher carbohydrate content, and, because many are made specifically for hypoallergenic purposes, they often do not contain corn. One choice I would recommend for this purpose is Natural Balance Vegetarian Dog Food (no corn, moderate to low protein).

Although it is controversial, it may be useful in some cases to follow each regular meal within a couple of hours with a small pure carbohydrate meal, containing as little protein as possible. It has been suggested that this might increase production of serotonin by the brain, with benefits on the dog's mood. Ingredients to consider might include white, long-grain, instant or parboiled rice, pasta, carrots and bananas. These foods are low in protein and high in starch. The carbohydrate meal should include a B-complex vitamin, or specifically a vitamin B6 at 1 mg/kg bodyweight/day. A folicin supplement and a vitamin B12 supplement may also be helpful. Ground flaxseeds added to the mix can provide a rich source of omega-3 fatty acids, which may also have a beneficial effect on mood, and hence behavior. Regardless of whether you change your dog's diet in this way, the dog should preferably be on a high-quality diet. When checking the label, rice, sweet potato, oats or barley are preferable to corn. If the dog is not currently on such a diet, switch her to the new diet gradually, over 10 days. For example, starting with 90% of the old diet and 10% of the new, increase the percentage of the new diet by 10% each day until the dog is on 100% of the new diet. This will prevent stomach upset and diarrhea. A properly formulated home-cooked diet is preferable to commercial kibble, with variety built into the diet where feasible, but this should be formulated by a qualified nutrition consultant or veterinary nutritionist (http://www.PetDiets.com). Otherwise, consider using a top-quality kibble.

### Mental Enrichment

When a dog is engaged in active mental effort, she is less likely to be emotional. You should therefore give some thought to adding some enjoyable mental stimulation to the dog's life. Following are some ideas for increasing mental stimulation in dogs. If the dog uses aggressive behaviors because she is generally risk averse, extra care needs to be taken about which mental enrichment exercises are recommended.

- Feed meals in a Buster® Cube or similar puzzle ball. This will allow the dog to work at getting her food.
- Hide some portion of meals around the house in small piles. This will encourage the dog to forage.
- Engage the dog in training. This can be toward formal obedience, or a canine sport such as agility, flyball or freestyle. As long as the dog enjoys the training, it will inhibit problematic emotions, such as fear and anxiety. Make it challenging but still lots of fun. I highly recommend clicker training (see the description of free shaping, below).
- Take road trips. Visiting new places for a hike or some other activity can be stimulating for most dogs.
- Use free shaping! Free shaping involves training a new behavior by reinforcing closer and closer approximations to the behavior without doing anything to prompt the behavior. It is like a game of hot and cold. Free shaping training engages the dog and actively encourages her to use flexible, experimental approaches to gain access to reinforcers. Dogs who are free shaped are more resilient and flexible in their behavior and are less impulsive and behaviorally rigid. In my experience, they are less affected by problematic emotionality. Free shaping usually involves use of a clicker (a small device that makes a clicking sound) to "mark" the moment when the dog performed the desired behavior; the click is followed by a reinforcer, often a food treat. During free shaping, each time that you withhold the click-and-treat for a behavior, you are adding very small amounts of stress to the situation. Small amounts of manageable stress are quite beneficial to learning, and help the dog to learn valuable coping skills; the dog is empowered because her behavior is more successful under challenge. Free shaping is particularly good for dogs with problematic conditioned emotional responses because it promotes confidence. You can find instructions for free shaping in *Don't Shoot the Dog* by Karen Pryor.

### Medication

There are no magic happy pills, but there are some medications and nutritional supplements that may, in some cases, help minimize the incidence of aggression. Discuss your options with your veterinarian if you feel this might be an option you would like to explore. Medications have side effects and are not without risk, so they are not to be taken lightly, but they can sometimes be part of the answer. Prozac® or Reconcile™ (fluoxetine) is one medication that has been very helpful in aggression problems.

While not a medication, a readily available over-the-counter nutritional supplement worth considering is 5-HTP (5-hydroxytryptophan). It has been shown to be highly effective in moderating many behavior problems, including aggression, with far fewer or less problematic side effects than the heavy-duty prescription medications. It is surprising that veterinarians are not more familiar with this supplement, and that they do not take greater advantage of it, given its effectiveness, its relatively low cost and that it works as soon as it is taken (unlike many medications, which can take weeks to build up an effect). It should not be used in conjunction with medications that affect serotonin activity. The correct dosage is determined experimentally. If the dose is slightly high, the dog may be initially nauseous. If the dose is too low, no effects will be achieved. The dose used at Tufts University School of Veterinary Medicine for addressing aggression is 2 mg/kg, administered orally every 12 hours.

If 5-HTP is used, you should watch for signs of serotonin syndrome (caused by an excess of serotonin activity in the brain). These include confusion/disorientation, agitation/irritability, low responsiveness/coma, anxiety, hypomania (elevated mood and increased activity), lethargy and seizures (Sorenson, 2002). You should also be on the lookout for these signs with the use of medications that influence serotonin activity.

If your veterinarian is unfamiliar with 5-HTP, you can bring them this citation so they can look into it for you:

- Birdsall, T. C. (1998). 5-Hydroxytryptophan: A clinically-effective serotonin precursor. *Alternative Medical Review, 3(4)*, 271–280.

If it still available online, you can print the Birdsall article from: http://www.thorne.com/altmedrev/.fulltext/3/4/271.pdf

## What's Wrong with Aversives?

An aversive stimulus is anything that an individual acts to escape or avoid because it is painful, noxious or unpleasant. So, what's wrong with electrically shocking a dog for bad behavior, hitting her or even yelling at her, forcing her to remain in an unpleasant situation until she behaves more acceptably, or producing other unpleasant conditions for her in order to suppress her aggressive behaviors? Making use of aversive stimulation in training dogs has the effect of motivating behavior, but it also produces undesirable secondary effects, often referred to as "fallout." Following is an explanation of the side effects associated with aversive stimulation and why it is inadvisable to use this kind of stimulation in behavior change programs.

In order for punishments to work, you must meet stringent criteria. It is next to impossible to meet these criteria, and the cost of not meeting them is high. I will not coach you in these criteria because I don't want to encourage anyone to believe they can effectively meet them. Even professionals can rarely meet them. However, one criterion I would like to discuss to highlight this impossible challenge is the magnitude of the aversive.

The intensity or magnitude of the aversive stimulus must be high enough to suppress the behavior completely but not so intense as to cause serious psychological trauma. Each individual dog is different in terms of this narrow window of appropriate intensity, and each individual's window fluctuates on a minute-by-minute basis. Judging the appropriate intensity is extremely difficult, at best, and certainly impractical. The risk of choosing the inappropriate intensity is high. If you start with a mild aversive stimulus and ramp it up if it does not work, the animal habituates to it so that it is ineffective. The aversive stimulus should be abrupt and intense to work—the higher the intensity, the greater the suppression of the behavior. The problem, of course, is that intense aversive stimulation creates fallout (see below). As well, choosing an initial high intensity is unethical, since we strive for the least aversive and intrusive methods.

Meeting the criteria for effective use of punishment is for all intents and purposes impossible in the real world and, when you fail to meet them, serious behavioral problems are likely to result. Furthermore, it is not certain that meeting all the criteria perfectly eliminates the fallout risk.

## Side Effects

What is the fallout that can take place when you make use of aversive stimulation? The most prominent effects are social disruption, aggression and countercontrol. These effects can occur even if you do come close to meeting the criteria alluded to above. If your punishments are noncontingent (that is, the punishment sometimes occurs regardless of whether the behavior occurred immediately beforehand), you are also likely to cause some level of learned helplessness or disempowerment. These common side effects are briefly discussed below.

## Social Disruption

Unpleasant experiences can disrupt and degrade social relationships. As we have seen, respondent conditioning is always taking place. When you (the dog's guardian) become associated with unpleasant experiences—and the more unpleasant, the stronger will be the association—you will come to elicit the fear and anxiety associated with the pain or unpleasantness. The social bond between you and your dog deteriorates. Furthermore, harsh aversive techniques do not usually suppress just the target behavior; they inhibit all behavior. The dog begins to behave as little as possible altogether and loses her spontaneity. When she does behave, she tends to do so in a rigid and safe fashion rather than a fun and experimental fashion. Unfortunately, global behavioral suppression is desirable for many guardians, and so their harsh behaviors are reinforced when the dog's behavior is suppressed.

## Aggression

Aversive stimulation provokes both lashing-out-type aggression and more goal-directed aggressive behavior. The longer the aversive stimulation lasts, the more probable is an aggressive reaction. Upon being aversively stimulated, animals will even attack inanimate objects if live individuals are not available. Since aversives are, by definition, something we act to escape or avoid and since aggressive behaviors are the usual way animals escape or avoid something (at least when flight is not possible or has not been a successful strategy in the past), aversives are clearly not appropriate when trying to resolve aggression problems. Using methods that tend to provoke aggressive behavior in order to change aggressive behavior is usually counterproductive.

## Countercontrol

Related to the notion of social disruption is "countercontrol." Countercontrol occurs when individuals learn how to "control their controllers." Invariably, subjects of aversive stimulation will countercontrol their environment, including the people who are the source of the aversive stimulation. Some people interpret the dog's countercontrol behavior as "dominant" behavior. They may use this as a reason to make further use of aversive strategies to regain dominance over the dog. This creates a vicious cycle that degrades the relationship between dog and human and often results in longstanding behavior problems or euthanasia of the dog.

## Learned Helplessness

If aversive stimulation is used without being contingent on the dog's behavior, and the aversive stimulation seems inescapable to the dog, the result can be various degrees of learned helplessness. Learned helplessness occurs when animals faced with an inescapable noncontingent aversive simply shut down. They will stop trying to find a way to escape even when the option to escape is subsequently made readily available. These dogs have simply given up and resigned themselves to the seeming fact that they cannot escape. This is a very sad state of affairs. People who use aversives often think they are meeting the requirement for contingency when, in fact, they are delivering the aversive more on the basis of their mood at the time rather than the specific behaviors of the dog. Learned helplessness is the polar opposite of empowerment, a state of confidence in one's ability to operate on one's environment effectively and to gain access to reinforcers. While empowerment is conducive to psychological wellbeing, learned helplessness is its antithesis.

## But Does Punishment Work?

By definition, punishment "works"—it is a truism. Punishment is defined as stimulation that results in a decline in the frequency or magnitude of a behavior. If an aversive stimulus does not produce a decline in behavior, it is not punishment. If it does produce a decline in behavior, it is punishment. Under this definition, we must conclude that punishment works. So, if all of the appropriate conditions are met, a severe aversive stimulation may, in some cases, permanently suppress a behavior.

However, in the vast majority of cases in dog training (outside of an artificial laboratory situation), the appropriate conditions are not met, and punishment is usually ineffective in the long run. Aside from its challenges, it is just not as likely to work as well as a positive-reinforcement-based approach. If a behavior is reinforced even occasionally, the target behavior will only be briefly suppressed by punishment, rather than eliminated. As soon as punishment is discontinued, the behavior recovers quickly. In a pragmatic sense of the word "works," which takes into account the long-term incidence of the behavior, the emotional consequences of the aversive stimulation, and the difficulty of avoiding side effects, we may conclude that the use of aversives does not "work." It may work to temporarily suppress a particular behavior, but in the long run, it usually causes more harm than good.

Part of the problem with punishment is that it fails to address the reason the behavior exists. Reinforcement drives behavior. If we are focused on trying to suppress behaviors, we are fussing about around the edges of the problem and not with the problem itself—it is just plain inefficient. The vastly more efficient approach is to identify the reinforcers driving any given behavior and manipulate those. If we are punishing a behavior and the reinforcement is left unaddressed, the dog will simply find another way to access the reinforcer or will go right back to the problem behavior once punishment is discontinued. The dog will figure out a way to work around you. As we have seen, most aggressive behaviors are maintained by the dog's desire to escape or avoid something. Punishing these behaviors certainly does not remove the motivation to avoid or escape that thing; in fact, it often increases that motivation. It is far better to identify the reinforcer maintaining the problem behavior and allow the dog to access that reinforcer (or a better one) by using a more desirable behavior instead. Furthermore, you address the fears by associating the whole situation with good things and you carry it out gradually, so you are able to teach the dog that an alternative choice will work out better for them than the aggressive behaviors did. You arrange the environment so that the dog chooses the desirable behavior.

I should note that negative reinforcement is one technique that uses aversive stimulation but does address the reinforcement for the behaviors involved. For example, this might involve exposing the dog to a scary situation and then allowing her to escape from the situation when she performs a desirable behavior. However, negative reinforcement, like positive punishment, involves an aversive stimulation. For those opposed to using aversives, there is rarely a situation where they would choose to implement a negative-reinforcement-based procedure over a positive-reinforcement-based procedure.

In summary, the answer to the question, "Does aversive stimulation and/or punishment-based training work?" depends on one's definition for "works." Most of the evidence suggests that punitive methods simply do not tend to "work" well in the real world in an all-things-considered sense of the term. Instead, be creative. Find a way to change the environment such that the dog is not likely to perform aggressive behaviors and then gradually install a replacement behavior, making that alternative really worth the dog's while, which will simultaneously countercondition fearful emotional responses. That's the key. Aversives are not going to get you where you want to be in your relationship with your dog.

## Putting it All Together

You might feel a little lost at this point, so let me try to bring together much of what we have explored so far. Briefly, we have talked about why dogs aggress and we have reviewed the basic principles of behavior. We have looked at how to assess the problem you are facing and describe in a useful manner the behaviors you want to change. You should now have a good solid contingency statement describing the behavior and its antecedents and consequences. We have also described some of the most powerful behavior change procedures (systematic desensitization and behavior replacement). Now I would like to help put this all together so you can construct a plan of action, a behavior change program (as it is called in behavior analysis).

First, is the problem behavior motivated by fear? Is the dog's motivation to escape or avoid something? Does some stimulus get removed as a result of the behavior? If so, then that stimulus is obviously unpleasant for the dog, and her behavior is being maintained by negative reinforcement. This means that we will need to address her fear in order to get at the root of the problem. Even if the dog looks offensive and confident, that does not mean she is. Sometimes dogs will look fearful and sometimes they will not. Being offensive and confident looking is simply the behavior that has worked best for her (acting fearful is not usually very successful at making humans stay away). It does not mean she is a stone-cold sociopathic killer, just that appeasement behaviors and fleeing have not worked as well as offensive-looking behavior in allowing her to escape or avoid the problem thing. The more emotional the behavior is, the more important it will be not just to address the operant behaviors but also to get at those emotions and change them—in other words, countercondition them. Of course, even if fear is motivating the behavior, there are obviously operants involved too. Otherwise, there would not be aggression. The lunging, snarling, snapping, biting etc. are operants, and as such they are driven by their consequences. So, you do not determine what is maintaining the behavior solely by whether the dog looks fearful or not; you determine it by whether the behavior allows her to access something, on the one hand, or to escape or avoid something, on the other hand.

Alternatively, if the behavior lacks emotionality (it is maintained by positive reinforcement, rather than negative reinforcement) and is a simple matter of the dog using aggressive behaviors to access a reinforcer of some kind because she has learned that this is the most effective way to do so, then you do not need to incorporate counterconditioning into the plan. In that case, a straight behavior replacement plan is the way to go. Teach the dog that aggressive behaviors will not work but something else will instead (see the section on extinction).

In the vast majority of cases, aggressive behavior does involve fear and sometimes frustration. Addressing the fear is pretty straightforward. The dog currently experiences fear in relation to the problem thing, and, as a result, she uses aggressive behaviors to escape or avoid it. Respondents and operants are involved here, so we need to address both. She does what works to get her what she wants. We will change what she wants and how she will get what she wants.

Frustration comes from being blocked from achieving some goal. The dog is emotional because she is being prevented from doing what she wants. In these cases, you need to be creative. You will want to teach the dog a more acceptable way to get what she wants. In some cases, the dog may want something that you simply cannot provide, but perhaps you can try to satisfy the dog's needs in other ways.

Where frustration or simple desire leads a dog to try to access a reinforcer, and positive reinforcement maintains that aggressive behavior, try not to allow the dog to get that reinforcer if she does aggress. On the flip side, make a more acceptable behavior work well, if not to get that exact reinforcer, then to get something else that is similar or of high value. That is, teach the dog that aggressive behaviors will not work (extinguish the aggressive behavior) but something else will instead (positively reinforce a more acceptable behavior). In behavior analysis, we call that procedure differential reinforcement (of other, alternative or incompatible behavior).

Protocols do not necessarily have to address only operant conditioning or only respondent conditioning as might have been suggested by my description of the procedures in their pure form. Most protocols that I design in the real world for cases involving prominent fear responses include techniques from both approaches and take advantage of the benefits that each provides. Think about the similarities and differences between the two approaches:

| Similarities | Differences |
|---|---|
| • Incremental, gradual exposure to the problem thing from less intense to more intense. | • Pair the problem thing with pleasant things to change the emotion (respondent conditioning) versus reinforcing desirable behaviors with pleasant consequences (operant conditioning). |
| • Prevent the dog from becoming fearful or from aggressing. | |

We can allow for the differences and include the similarities in the same protocol in order to get the benefits from both. We can change problem emotional associations and reinforce more desirable behaviors in the same procedure.

Usually, the same stimulus that elicits the problem emotional response also evokes the aggressive behaviors. So, that is where we start. Use your antecedent control procedures to minimize the odds of an aggressive display. Now figure out the steps for exposing the dog to the problem thing in small steps. You'll want to remain flexible, but it is useful to have this list as a guideline. For instance, you might have the dog in place and bring the problem thing to a distance at which she notices it but is not yet likely to respond aggressively. This is where the procedure would change if we chose only respondent or only operant conditioning. The focus in systematic desensitization is to present the fear-eliciting thing (strangers, say) and then the pleasure-eliciting thing (treats, play etc.). So: stranger enters, treats start flowing, stranger leaves, treats stop flowing, repeat, and on and on at successive levels of exposure. The emotional response should change from "Oh no, strangers; she's going to try and hurt me" to "Yippy, strangers! Treats are coming." The operant approach would be different. You would bring the stranger in and then either cue a specific behavior or reinforce anything other than aggressive or fearful behaviors. In either case, stranger enters, nonaggressive behaviors are performed, treats are delivered, stranger leaves, treats stop flowing. Can you see how you might get both types of conditioning in if you are careful? Do you see how the fun and games that are used to reinforce prosocial behaviors are also being paired with the stranger? Counterconditioning (changing the problem emotional response to a desirable emotional response) is a byproduct of doing your behavior replacement procedure, as long as you ensure that the dog does not aggress or become excessively fearful and that you use pleasure-eliciting stimuli such as high-value treats, play or attention. Now you have the key to constructing your behavior change program. Look over your notes and contingency statement, decide whether emotional responses are present and then construct your procedure, writing out the hierarchy and target behaviors. Move toward having a dog who responds appropriately when faced with the previously problematic stimulus.

In summary then, dogs do what works to get them what they want. Our goal, if what they want is to escape or avoid something (as a result of fear), is to change what they want (make it so they like, rather than fear, the "thing"). Whether fear motivates the aggressive behaviors or not, we also need to arrange the environment (antecedents and consequences) so that the dog chooses to perform some other, more acceptable behavior instead of aggressive behaviors. To achieve all of this, we gradually and incrementally expose the dog to the problem stimulus (maintaining the dog subthreshold throughout), pairing it with pleasure-eliciting things and reinforcing desirable behaviors. We simultaneously change the emotional response, thereby changing what the dog wants (approach rather than escape/avoid), and change what works to get them what they want (prosocial rather than aggressive behaviors). We change the antecedent to elicit more pleasurable emotional responses and evoke behaviors that are more desirable, and we change the consequences to make choosing prosocial behaviors the more valuable choice.

## Then What? (Generalization and Maintenance)

Once you have worked through your behavior change program and have carried out the procedures to a point where you are making significant progress and are happy with the result, the process is not over. Once you have achieved your initial goals, you need to work on generalizing the results and maintaining them in the long term. Dogs who use aggressive behaviors often revert to those behavioral strategies if they come up against something new—a new environment or a variation on the problem thing. You want to teach the dog that the rules you have taught her apply not just to one or two narrow situations, but universally, in all situations. Dogs don't generalize these lessons as well as we might like, so you specifically have to cover them. That means carrying out the exercises in a variety of environments so that the dog learns that the same contingencies are in place even if the situation is a bit different. If the program involved strangers, you will need to carry out the procedure with a wide variety of strangers, all different in some ways and in different places. If it involves stepping over the dog, then you want her to learn that this means anyone stepping over her, not just you; perhaps a toe grazes her sometimes. Once you have helped the behavior generalize to various environments, you need to refresh the dog's memory from time to time. Ensure that you regularly reinforce her for making the right choice. Once a dog has been aggressive, you really need to keep a close eye on her behavior permanently. Don't slip into complacency.

# CHAPTER 6. STRATEGIES FOR COMMON SCENARIOS

This chapter presents some general strategies and sample protocols for dealing with common aggressive behavior scenarios. It is *not* to be confused with cookie-cutter "treatments" for generic categories of aggression. I present common scenarios and distinctions, but any behavior change program must address the specific antecedents, behaviors and consequences of a particular case. The general strategies and sample protocols presented here should serve only to illustrate application of the principles and procedures of behavior change. They should stimulate creativity, not stifle it with the suggestion that these are the only or best approaches, or that these protocols should be applied unchanged for all similar cases.

## On-Leash Aggressive Behaviors

It is common for dogs to learn to make use of aggressive behaviors on leash. When dogs are on leash, their options to escape or avoid something are limited, and aggressive behavior becomes more effective as an option than flight. In some instances, the dog can develop a problematic emotional response from the reaction of the guardian; for example, the guardian might tighten the leash and show other avoidance behaviors. Often, the dog is afraid of something because she was not well socialized to it as a puppy, or because she had an early traumatic experience with that thing. Furthermore, some guardians inadvertently reinforce aggressive behaviors with what they believe or intend to be "punishment." Otherwise, guardians might negatively reinforce aggressive behavior by increasing the distance between the dog and the evoking stimulus when the dog acts aggressively.

The first step is to consider antecedent control procedures. This includes changing the way things are done, preventing exposure to the evoking stimuli, and perhaps increasing the effort required to act aggressively by using a head halter, such as a Gentle Leader[2]. Avoid creating unnecessary tension on the leash and consider whether a basket muzzle is necessary.

---

[2] Many dogs dislike head halters. If your dog finds this unpleasant, you have to decide whether to use it or not. If you feel you really need it, then desensitize the dog to it gradually and only use it in your protocols when and if the dog comes to like it; otherwise you will be violating the principle of using only pleasant stimulation and going into the protocols with the dog relaxed.

The operants involved in on-leash aggressive behavior are usually maintained by the consequence of escape or avoidance. You should implement a program of reinforcing other, alternative or incompatible behavior in place of the problem behaviors. If fear is a component, be sure to use systematic desensitization as well.

Some cases of on-leash aggressive behaviors are maintained by positive reinforcement. This can occur when guardians try to countercondition the dog's emotional response. By feeding the dog treats while she is aggressing, the guardian may inadvertently reinforce the aggressive behaviors. Another possibility is that the guardian creates a "behavior chain," in which the dog aggresses in order to access the opportunity to perform another behavior that is then positively reinforced. The latter problem often results from the guardian attempting to "redirect" or distract the dog. For example, the dog aggresses, the guardian requests a sit or eye contact and then, once the dog sits or makes eye contact, the guardian positively reinforces that behavior. The dog learns to aggress in order to obtain the opportunity to sit or make eye contact and be reinforced. The difference between this scenario and the behavior replacement strategy we have been discussing is that, in this accidental behavior chain, the dog aggresses, whereas in the behavior replacement strategy, the dog does not and therefore the chain cannot be learned. Always be on the lookout for this possibility when you are assessing the consequences of your dog's aggressive behavior. For effective behavior change programming, it is vital to know what maintains the behavior.

Many people have had great success with training the dog to watch them instead of the other dog or person, or otherwise look away from the problem stimulus. The tunnel attention on the problem stimulus that can occur under stressful situations contributes to increasing the dog's arousal until aggressive behavior occurs. Breaking this tunnel attention is one way of preventing arousal from escalating and thus averting the problem behaviors. Remember that the dog makes these choices voluntarily, based on the history of reinforcement for each choice. The dog interacts with the environment, including the aversive stimulus, and the goal is to arrange the contingencies such that it becomes more worthwhile for the dog to look away to the guardian than to erupt in displays of aggressive behavior. It is not about preventing the dog from interacting with the aversive stimulus, but rather making it worth her while to respond to that stimulus with a less problematic set of behaviors. In fact, it will also be about making the stimulus less scary so the dog feels less need to escape or avoid it to begin with. The key is that it is the dog's choice to behave otherwise. In many cases, reinforcement of any other behavior is used; that is, any calm, nonaggressive behavior is targeted for positive reinforcement. In the end, this usually results in shaping looking away, even if this was not the specific behavior targeted.

In order to carry out this particular strategy, you should start by preventing the dog from aggressing while you work on training a solid look-away or look-at-handler cue (which also helps prevent a behavior chain from being inadvertently trained). Once the training is good and solidly reliable, it is time to move to the next stage.

In their excellent book, *Feisty Fido: Help for the Leash-Aggressive Dog*, McConnell and London (2003) suggest the "autowatch." This refers to transferring the cue for looking at the handler from a verbal cue to the presentation of the aversive stimulus; in other words, the arrival of the "stranger" cues the dog to watch you rather than you having to request this behavior. This is called transferring stimulus control. In order to transfer stimulus control from one stimulus to another, you repeatedly present the *new* stimulus (the approaching stranger, say), followed immediately by the *old* stimulus (the verbal cue you have trained for that behavior). This evokes the behavior, which is followed immediately by the reinforcer. In this case, you present the stranger and then give the verbal cue for eye contact, then reinforce eye contact with treats or a play session. After a number of repetitions, the appearance of the stranger will control the behavior and the verbal cue will not be needed. Note that the dog does not aggress in this sequence and so the behavior chain problem that was discussed above will not develop.

McConnell and London (2003) also suggest training an "emergency U-turn" and solid sit-and-make-eye-contact for situations that cannot be avoided in which the dog will otherwise be accidentally provoked. Clearly, a solid sit-and-make-eye-contact could be valuable in cases where an off-leash dog charges you and your dog-aggressive dog. The emergency U-turn is for situations in which you are caught off guard and the provocative stimulus just seems to pop out of nowhere. It is most effective to train the dog to U-turn immediately before she aggresses, rather than after. You should decide ahead of time which protocol to use if the dog does aggress. My recommendation is to observe carefully for initial signs that the dog is becoming less relaxed, and disengage as soon as you can. You should recognize this event as an error in the training program and endeavor to avoid it next time.

In some cases, the dog who is motivated by escape/avoidance makes less use of aggressive behaviors like lunging, snapping and biting, and uses more flight or appeasement behaviors, such as withdrawal, before resorting to active tactics when cornered; the dog may also seem to be experiencing a significant emotional response. In these cases, I would design a program that would achieve respondent conditioning at the same time as training the new behavior. This would involve antecedent control and replacement of the aggressive behavior with an incompatible behavior, using incremental, graded exposure to the problem stimulus. If possible, the program should make use of volunteer set-ups, which are easier to control than the "real world," followed by controlled real-life set-ups after some progress has been made.

You should observe some general guidelines while working on-leash with the dog. Avoid tightening the leash when approaching or passing other people or dogs. A tightened leash sends the signal to the dog that you are tense, and can actually come to serve as a cue to aggress, thus contributing to the problem. On the other hand, if keeping the leash loose is just too challenging, I have trained dogs to look away for reinforcement cued by light tension on the leash (that is, tightening the leash cues the dog to look or walk away). More than one cue can be used for the same behavior; that is, looking away can be cued by both the problem stimulus and independently by tightening the leash.

Another general guideline is that you should act calm or happy, never tense, nervous or upset. Being relaxed means breathing normally, having loose muscles, walking freely and smoothly, speaking in a gentle or happy tone and having a gentle smile. Being tense means breathing irregularly, having tense muscles and a serious or distressed look on your face, tightening the leash, speaking in a concerned or scared tone, consoling the dog, becoming upset with the dog and walking stiffly and quickly. Fake relaxation or exaggerated happiness is not helpful. Pay close attention to the signals you are sending out to ensure that you are not contributing to the dog's tension.

If the dog–dog on-leash aggressive dog has not been well socialized with other dogs, you might be able to improve her social behavior with other dogs using remedial socialization. In a section below (page 116), I outline procedures for setting up remedial socialization between dogs to encourage affiliative interactions and appropriate social behaviors.

## Location-Related Aggressive Behaviors

The so-called "territorial" aggressive dog uses aggressive behaviors when strangers enter, or even merely approach, the dog's "territory." The dog's territory usually means the house and yard. Location-related aggression is usually maintained by negative reinforcement; it functions to ward off strangers. Often, the initial provocative stimulus is a knock at the door or ringing of the doorbell, although some dogs are able to see or hear strangers approach. In some cases, aggressive displays are positively reinforced by guardians. This reinforcement is often inadvertent; guardians intend their actions as punishment or as calming to the aggressive display. As always, the label of "territorial aggression" is not enough because it does not identify what is maintaining the behavior in a particular case; a proper functional assessment identifies the specific antecedents and consequences influencing the specific behaviors involved.

Working with these dogs often requires some creativity and flexibility. In many cases, use of creative antecedent control procedures can make a significant difference. Feeding a low-protein diet, supplemented with 5-HTP, may significantly reduce location-related aggression. Focus on practices that increase the activity of serotonin in the brain. This might involve more exercise, and, if the problem is intense or intractable, Prozac might be appropriate. If the dog is able to see strangers approaching, adjusting furniture or drapes may be enough to solve the problem. In other instances, changing the placement of the dog's bed, so that it is away from the window or door, can reduce the dog's ability to hear people approaching. Putting the mailbox at the street instead of at the door can be helpful, as can putting up a sign requesting no unsolicited visitors or peddlers. If the problem occurs primarily when you or other family members are not present, you can play the radio while you are out in order to make other sounds less obvious. If the dog aggresses from behind a chain-link fence, a solid fence can solve the problem, or the dog can be kept inside. In many cases, remedial socialization is also useful. Being creative with antecedent control is often the best solution to these kinds of problems.

My generally preferred approach to this problem, aside from antecedent control procedures, involves behavior replacement and counterconditioning. The more emotionality is involved, the more care I would take to ensure that counterconditioning is a prominent part of the plan. In some cases, you may merely want the dog out of the way to greet guests. In others, the situation really calls for counterconditioning. One of my most successful protocols involves training the dog to go to a specific place, cued by the doorbell and/or a knock at the door. You can start by training a solid placement command, so that the dog goes to a specific place on cue. Then you can transfer stimulus control from the verbal cue to the doorbell (remember the sequence: new cue, old cue, behavior, reinforcement). One trick I have learned is to start the training with a brand new bell ring, getting rid of the old bell. The old ring sound was a discriminative stimulus ("trigger") for aggressive behaviors. It is better to start fresh with a new stimulus for the placement training to avoid having to extinguish the response to the original bell first. As described below, training should be done incrementally, keeping the dog below her threshold for aggressive behavior and ensuring that she is repeatedly successful. These repeated successes will also countercondition the dog's emotional reaction.

Use very special treats, toys or a game and really make it worth the dog's while to sit quietly beside you at the door to greet guests, or to go to a crate or another room when the bell rings. Once the dog is sitting quietly beside you or going to a specific place when family members arrive, trials can be arranged to work with acquaintances and friends, and finally with strangers. You should work gradually, not increasing the level of difficulty until the dog is eagerly anticipating visitors at each level. In some cases, this process of behavior replacement with counterconditioning when visitors arrive may be sufficient. In others, it may also be necessary to countercondition the dog's response to guests actually inside the house. Many dogs use aggressive displays only until a person is actually in the house, but some remain leery of guests inside the house. Counterconditioning can be useful in these cases.

The process of counterconditioning requires volunteers. I recommend at least one visitor per day. If you can arrange for 10 visitors every day, however, the program will progress much more rapidly and smoothly. You may have to use a muzzle through many of these exercises to ensure that everyone remains safe. If a muzzle is used, you should try the exercise without the muzzle only after you have run through the program with one and everything has gone smoothly. If you have removed the muzzle, you should attach a leash so that you can regain control of the dog if she aggresses.

You should ask the visitor to ignore the dog for the first couple of minutes, only greeting the dog after that and only if she is calm and quiet. Greetings should be low key and not threatening. That means letting the dog sniff the visitor and perhaps take a treat. Quick movements by the visitor or pats on the top of the head should be avoided, at least at first.

The rule for the counterconditioning component is (as always) as follows: when strangers are present, the fun and games start, and when strangers are not present, the fun and games stop. The aim is to have the stranger come to predict the fun and games. You should be a little on the boring side except when visitors are arriving and present so that there is an obvious contrast between the two situations. Contrast and repetition are key. You need to pay close attention to the dog's arousal level. If the fun and games are promoting a problematic level of arousal, you will have to tone it down, focusing on things that create a pleasant experience without promoting aggressive behaviors and arousal. Often, gentle praise and yummy treats are sufficient.

You should reinforce for calmness, thereby starting the association between visitor and fun, as well as increasing the frequency of calm behaviors. Visitors who are unlikely to cause any reactivity (perhaps friends and nonresident family members whom the dog already likes) can be used first, working up to unknown guests. When the visitor arrives, all the fun and games start. Then a few minutes later the visitor leaves and so do all the fun and games. This is repeated until the dog is visibly eager to have the guest arrive. Arousal levels can be managed by taking breaks when necessary, and the session should always end on a positive note. These visits should be set up as exercises, lasting 5 minutes each.

Once the process is going smoothly, you should be able to get the visitors involved, having them participate in the fun and games. To begin with, this might involve having the visitor tossing a treat gently to the dog, but eventually the visitor should be able to hand the treats to the dog or play fetch down the hallway with a favored toy. The visitor could bring a new toy or the best treats with them. It is important to ensure that the dog does not use aggressive behaviors to guard valuable resources (such as food and toys) before doing these protocols.

Visitors should avoid directly facing the dog, leaning over her or staring at her. Instead, they should face slightly away from her and approach in an arc, rather than walking in a straight line towards her. Approaching a dog in an arc is less threatening, and is one of the rituals that strange dogs use with one another. Even better, particularly at first, is to not approach the dog at all but allow her to come to the visitor of her own volition. Averted eyes will also be helpful in defusing a tense situation. The treat can be handed to the dog or tossed from the side (no sudden movements, though).

This protocol should, over time, create a beneficial emotional response to strangers. The goal is to have this reaction generalize to all strangers with repetition. The dog will come to anticipate games and treats when visitors show up; visitors will be a "good thing." The process takes a significant amount of time and effort, careful micromanagement and good judgment.

# Guarding Behaviors

Object guarding is easy to understand. Using aggressive behavior in order to avoid having a valued object removed is common, and adaptive. Since the dog already has access to the object in question and the aggressive behavior functions to dissuade others from approaching and/or removing the object, the behavior is maintained by negative reinforcement. *Mine! A Practical Guide to Resource Guarding in Dogs* by Jean Donaldson is an excellent book for those who are experiencing this problem.

My general strategy for resource guarding is to use behavior replacement procedures and counterconditioning, with incremental graded exposure in order to set the dog up for success. Antecedent control procedures are often helpful. However, my experience has been that guarding is strongly influenced by the dog's learning that the approach of others is aversive because it reduces the dog's access to reinforcers. This contingency is what must change.

One option is to simply remove the object that the dog guards. In some cases, this is plausible, but in other cases—particularly if the guarded object is a person—it is not. Removal of the object may result in the dog choosing another object to guard. The dog has learned the general strategy of using aggressive behaviors to guard objects, and this behavior readily generalizes to other objects. She has also learned that the approach of others when reinforcers are present results in reduced access to reinforcers.

The sections below provide some advice for some common types of guarding behavior. As with all of the sample protocols in this chapter, behavior change programs must be constructed on the basis of the facts of the case. The steps identified here should only be considered generic examples.

## Food Bowl Guarding

- Set the dog up for success. Start the exercises with the person who provokes the least possessiveness, and generalize to others later.

- Have the dog tethered to a wall, if necessary, near her empty food bowl. Approach the bowl as closely as possible without having the dog become tense, drop or toss a valued treat into the bowl if she is not aggressing in any way, and walk away.

- Repeat this procedure, reinforcing calm tolerance each time. If you were only able to perform the exercises at a specific distance (say, 10 feet), then you can inch closer each time. Perform the exercises with approaches from different directions to help generalization. Once one person has performed some of the exercises, have other family members repeat them.

- Still with an empty bowl, approach, bend over half way to the bowl, drop in some treats and walk away. Because the bowl is empty, the dog should have no trouble with this. At the same time, she is learning how this game works: when you approach, she gets great treats if she is not aggressive, and gets nothing if she is (as always, try to arrange it so that she does not aggress). After several of these exercises, work on different angles as before.

- Still with an empty bowl, approach, bend over the bowl as you might if you were going to pick it up, but do not touch it. Pause and drop in a great treat or two, then walk away. Repeat several times and then add in some different angles. Only proceed to the next level when the dog is visibly eager to have you carry out the task. This will help ensure that counterconditioning occurs.

- Still with the bowl empty, approach, bend over and reach for the bowl as if to pick it up. Touch the bowl and then drop a few great treats in and walk away. Repeat several times and then add in some different angles.

- Still with an empty bowl, approach, bend over, reach for the bowl and touch it, then pause for a few seconds. Drop a few treats in the bowl and walk away. Repeat several times and then add in some different angles.

- Still with the bowl empty, approach, bend over, grasp the bowl and pick it up an inch off the ground. Immediately drop in a few great treats, put the bowl down and walk away. Repeat several times and then add in some different angles.

- Still with the bowl empty, approach, bend over, pick up the bowl a little further and pause an extra couple of seconds. Drop a few treats into the bowl, put it back down and walk away. Repeat several times and then add in some different angles.

- Still with the bowl empty, approach, bend over, pick up the bowl and stand upright. Immediately place a few treats in the bowl, place it back on the ground and walk away. Repeat several times and then add in some different angles.

- Still with the bowl empty, approach, bend over, pick up the bowl, carry it to a nearby counter, place treats in it and return it to the ground, then walk away. Repeat several times and then add in some different angles.

Assuming that the dog has no problem with being touched (other than in association with food), we can now start working on the other angle with food bowl issues: being touched, as opposed to having the food bowl itself touched. These steps are all about setting the dog up for success and helping her generalize the learning.

- Still with the bowl empty, approach, pat the dog on the back once (let her see you coming, no surprises), place a treat in the bowl and walk away. Repeat several times and then add in some different angles.

- Still with the bowl empty, approach, pat the dog a couple of times on the back, place a treat in the bowl and walk away. Repeat several times and then add in some different angles.

- Still with the bowl empty, approach, pat the dog a few times, drop a treat in the bowl and walk away. Repeat several times and then add in some different angles.

- Still with the bowl empty, approach, pat the dog numerous times, drop a treat in the bowl and walk away. Repeat several times and then add in some different angles.

At this stage, the dog can be asked to sit as you approach her and the food bowl.

Next, repeat the exercises above with food in the bowl. Initially, this can be done at times when the dog is not as hungry as she might be right before a real meal. A dry kibble that is not as palatable as the dog's usual food could also be used. Usually, it takes dogs a couple of minutes to eat a bowl of food. For fast eaters, a large rock can be placed in the bowl so that the dog has to eat around it, allowing another minute or so of exercises to be fitted in. Each feeding will probably allow time for several steps, and the process is then continued at the next meal, starting at a few levels before where it left off. The treats being used should be very high value! Veggie burger pieces are often perfect for this.

It is important to avoid having the dog become frustrated by these exercises! The way to avoid frustration is simply to make it really worth her while; that means using treats that are much better than the food used for the meal, and observing the dog carefully so you do not repeat the exercise too many times.

Once the sequence has been completed using a meal of less palatable kibble (optional), repeat it again with the dog's regular, more palatable kibble. In order to be sure that the dog is ready for real-life "cold" trials, you could even repeat the sequence using an extra-special food in the bowl. This requires that a solid foundation has been set using the best possible treats.

Finally, other people in the household should run through the sequence as part of a generalization program. It should be much easier for the next person to go through the protocols because of the significant load of learning already in place. The aim is to make sure that the dog understands that the approach of any household member predicts good things (provided that she does not behave aggressively).

Children less than about 12 years of age should not run through these exercises on their own. An adult should do the exercises with them, and the dog should be tethered to a wall for safety. Children under 9 years should probably not perform the exercises at all under any circumstances. They should be trained not to approach the dog when she is eating, and this should be assured with careful adult supervision.

You need to maintain the conditioning you have established. You should make an effort to have everyone in the household randomly perform at least one or two different kinds of approaches to the dog's food bowl at least once weekly. In a household of three people, that would mean at least three to six approaches per week.

## Object Guarding

The principles for object guarding are the same as for food-bowl guarding. Only the application differs. You should make a list of guarded objects, and training should start with the least guarded object on the list. This should be an object that the dog likes enough to take and maintain contact with but has not guarded. If there are no objects that fit this description, a few sessions can be done with any object that the dog does not guard, just so that she gets the hang of the game, even though she may lose interest in the object during sessions. For the actual sessions, the aim should be to start with the least guarded object on the list, with the person in the household who provokes the least aggression, and at a time of day or in a situation when the dog is least likely to guard (for example, this might be after exercise). Other times and contexts can be used later, but initially, it is important to ensure success. The following exercises assume that you are using a clicker in your training.

- Train the dog to "leave it" on cue. This can be shaped by holding an object that the dog does not guard and reinforcing when the dog backs away from it. You might have to start by reinforcing successive approximations to backing away from the object. Eventually, you can work up to having the dog let go of objects she is holding in her mouth. Add a verbal cue. Do not train this with any objects that will evoke aggressive behavior. Also train the dog to "take it" by reinforcing the behavior of taking treats or unguarded objects only on cue.

- Approach the dog while she has possession of the unguarded object and request her to "leave it." When she drops the item, click and deliver a great treat. Then give the "take it" cue so that she can have the object back. Walk away. Repeat several times and then add in some different distances and angles for your approach and different durations for which the dog possesses the object. Ideally, you should only proceed to the next level when the dog is visibly eager to have you carry out the task at the current level.

- Do the same as above, but bend half way to the object once it is dropped, then stand back up, cue the dog to take it, and click and treat.

- Do the same as above, but bend the rest of the way down to the object once it is dropped, stand back up, cue the dog to take it, and click and treat.

- Do the same as above, but reach half way to the object once it is dropped, retract your hand, stand up, cue the dog to take it, and click and treat.

- Do the same as above, but reach the rest of the way, touching the object briefly, before retracting your hand, standing up, cueing the dog to take it, and clicking and treating.

- Do the same as above, but pick the object up about an inch, place it back down, stand up, cue the dog to take it, and click and treat.

- Do the same as above, but pick the object up, stand upright, place the object back on the ground, cue the dog to take it, and click and treat.

- Do the same as above, but keep possession of the object for several seconds before placing it back on the ground, cueing the dog to take it, and clicking and treating.

- This time, you have initial possession of the object. Approach the dog with it. Offer it to her to take; when she does, maintain contact with the object. Do not let go. Cue the dog to leave it. When she does, immediately click and treat, and give her the object. Walk away. Bribe (treat offered up front for the behavior, not after) only if you absolutely have to in order to get the item back.

- Do the same as above, but allow the dog to have contact with the object for a few more seconds before withdrawing it.

- Do the same as above, but let go of the object for a second before gently taking it back. As soon as the dog allows you to take it back, click and treat.

- Do the same as above, but increase the duration for which you relinquish possession of the object to a couple of seconds before gently taking it back.

- Do the same as above, but increase the duration for which you relinquish possession to several seconds.

- Do the same as above, but after you relinquish possession of the object, take a step back before stepping back in and gently removing the object.

- Do the same as above, but take a couple of steps back and increase the duration. You may find that you have to break the duration and the distance into separate steps. Increasing them both at once may make the dog tense; if that happens, modify the protocol so that you gradually increase duration alone while still remaining close. Once you have the duration up to, say, 30 seconds, you can then relax the duration and work on distance. For example, go back to 5 seconds and take one step back. Then 5 seconds and two steps back. Then after working these two variables separately, work them together.

- Approach the dog from a short distance when she already has possession of the object and gently remove it (perhaps using the "leave it" cue when you grasp the object). Immediately click and treat, return the object and walk away.

- Do the same as above, but approach from a greater distance when the dog has had the object slightly longer. Repeat this several times in different rooms, with different angles of approach and from different distances.

- Next, work on handling and possession. When the dog has possession of the object, approach and pat her gently on the back once, click and treat, and walk away. Do not try to offer the treat to the dog directly from your hand. This may be seen as an attempt to take the object. Although you have already worked on taking the object, touching the dog while she has possession might be too demanding at this stage. Instead, just drop the treat close to the dog and walk away.

- Do the same as above, but pat a couple of times.

- Do the same as above, but pat several times.

- Do the same as above, but stroke the dog a couple of times on the back.

- Do the same as above, but pat the dog once on the back of the neck.

- Do the same as above, but pat her a few times on the back of the neck.

- Do the same as above, but pat her several times on the back of the neck.

- Do the same as above, but stroke her a few times on the back of the neck.

- Do the same as above, but pat her once on the head.

- Do the same thing, but pat her a couple of times on the head.

- Do the same thing, but pat her a few times on the head.

- Do the same thing, but pat her several times on the head.

- Do the same thing, but stroke her on the head.

- Do the same as above, but pat once on the head and then request the dog to "leave it." Pick up the item and return it to the dog. Click and treat, and walk away. This step requires a bit of flexibility. It involves adding some of the exercises together. If you have a good, solid foundation, this should go smoothly. If it does not, try making it easier on the dog by patting and having her drop the object but allow her to take it back herself. Otherwise, go back a few levels and do some more work on the component parts before trying to add them together.

- Repeat the sequences using the next item on the list of guarded objects (that is, the second least guarded object). Generalize the training by performing it in different rooms, and approaching from different angles and distances. Repeat the exercises several times through a few sessions, and do not move on to the next level until the dog is delighted to have you perform the various exercises, indicating that counterconditioning has also been achieved.

- Repeat the exercises with the next item on the list, and then the next, until you have worked through all the items that the dog guards.

- Have each sequence repeated by each person in the household. Successive people should be able to work through much more smoothly and quickly. Although the process should not be rushed, if the path is paved with a great foundation, it should go quite smoothly for others because the dog has learned the game and the lesson is now being generalized to other people. If the dog was tethered through these exercises, each person should run through the protocols again without tethering. Make sure you have a solid foundation before doing this.

You should maintain the learning that you have established. Make an effort to have everyone in the household randomly perform at least one or two different kinds of object exercises at least once weekly. In a household of three people, this would mean at least three to six approaches per week.

## Location Guarding

A good list of the locations that the dog guards is essential. Common locations include couches, dog beds, under desks and in cars. A written description of the antecedents that are important for this particular dog is also required. Variables such as the angle of approach, distance of approach and who approaches may be evident to the keen observer. This information will help you and the behavior consultant design a better protocol. It may be advisable to run through the exercises with the dog wearing a muzzle first and then repeat them without the muzzle.

The first few sessions involve training the dog to touch her nose to your hand, a behavior called "targeting." This is done first in a location that the dog does not guard, and this training is then applied to the problem situations. The target training provides a tool to complete the exercises and helps the dog start to understand the game.

- In a location away from any guarded areas, present the palm of your hand near the dog's face. The dog will probably investigate it. If she touches it with her nose, click and treat. If not, you might have to click a close call or even a glance and then reinforce closer and closer approximations to touching until she does touch your hand.

- Once the dog is targeting your hand (touching it with her nose), only click and treat for touches that occur within, say, 8 seconds. If she does not touch within this time, pull your hand away, wait a few seconds without saying or doing anything and present your hand again.

- Next, only click and treat when the dog targets within 5 seconds.

- Next, only click and treat when the dog targets within 3 seconds.

- Start clicking only for the good ones, rather than clicking and treating all of them. This will encourage the dog to work a little harder and it will make the response more resilient (less susceptible to extinction).

- Continue working the exercise until the dog is eagerly touching your palm with her nose immediately you present it.

- Practice having the dog displace herself in order to target your hand. Stand a few feet away and present your hand. The dog will probably come to you to touch your hand in order to win her treat. Click and treat.

- Move a few feet away and repeat. Make sure you do not involve any locations she guards, but try having her go to and from specific places.

Once a nice, solid targeting response is in place, it is ready to be applied to a protocol for location guarding, as follows:

- Start with a place that the dog does not guard. Jean Donaldson offers a great tip in her book *Mine! A Practical Guide to Resource Guarding in Dogs*, suggesting that if a couch is problematic perhaps the couch cushion on the floor well away from the couch might work. If that is still too "hot" a location, use some other specific location. Now you can incorporate a verbal cue. Give the cue you wish to use for getting the dog in or on the location (e.g., "up you go," "get in") and then present your hand at the location. The verbal cue must come before you present your hand. When the dog targets the hand and hence enters the location, offer gentle praise rather than clicks and treats. Getting into the location is the easy part, and the higher value reinforcement should be saved for getting out of it. Once the dog is in the location, immediately give a cue for her to get off or out of the location and then target her to exit the location. When she does, click and treat. The dog will learn over several repetitions that the verbal cue means that she can earn treats by targeting your hand. After a few trials, the dog should respond to the verbal cue before you have a chance to present your hand for targeting. When this happens, you can start using just the verbal cue. If it does not happen soon, pause for a few seconds between giving the verbal cue and presenting your hand to give the dog a chance to respond to the verbal cue. If she does not, do some more trials with both before trying again.

- Do the same as above, but allow the dog to lie down in the location before targeting her out.

- Do the same as above, but allow the dog to settle down a bit more in the location. This can be variable, and you might have to adjust the protocol on the fly, but 20 seconds might be a good duration to aim for. Remember that the amount of settling of the dog in the location is important and should be worked with gradually.

- Do the same as above, but allow the dog to settle down and get a bit more comfortable in the location (say 30 seconds). If the dog does not really want to be in the location much at all and just leaves frequently, perhaps a slightly more attractive location is necessary. For example, if the location being used is a particular spot on the carpet, you could try placing a folded blanket there to make it slightly more comfortable, so that the dog will at least feel like remaining there when invited.

- Do the same as above, but increase the duration (say, to 45 seconds) that the dog is allowed to remain in the location before you target her off.

- Do the same thing, but allow the dog to settle in a bit more deeply (say, 60 seconds).

- Do the same as above, but increase the duration slightly (say, to a minute and a half), and in that time walk away and come back.

- Do the same as above, but walk out of sight briefly.

- Do the same as above, but increase the duration slightly (say, to 2 minutes).

- Target the dog to enter the location and allow her to settle down. Then approach her and pat her on the back once, withdraw, wait several seconds and then target her off.

- Do the same as above, but pat the dog a few times.

- Do the same as above, but stroke the dog on the back.

- Do the same as above, but pat the dog once on the back of the neck.

- Do the same as above, but pat the dog on the back of the neck a few times.

- Do the same as above, but stroke the dog on the back of the neck.

- Do the same as above, but pat the dog once on top of her head.

- Do the same as above, but pat the dog a few times on top of the head.

- Do the same as above, but stroke the dog on the head.

- Target the dog to the location. Once she has settled down, crouch down 5 feet away (this distance will be variable, based on the particular dog). Get up, wait several seconds and target the dog off. Click and treat.

- Do the same as above, but sit down, rather than merely crouching.

- Do the same as above, but sit a foot closer to the dog.

- Do the same thing again, but sit a foot closer to the dog. Repeat this process until you are right beside the dog. You might have to close the distance gradually once you start getting close to the dog.

- Do the same as above, but pat the dog on the back. Repeat several times. Then do some in which you pat a few times and then some in which you stroke the dog on the back.

- Do the same as above, but work the back of the neck.

- Do the same as above, but work the head area.

- Carry out this sequence of stages again, this time using the next location on the list (that is, the next least guarded location). Then repeat the levels for the next location on the list until you have finished working the most guarded location.

- Have another person in the household run through the sequence.

- Once everyone has completed the protocols, everyone should run through them again without the muzzle on the dog.

As before, be careful not to make the dog frustrated with this. Make it really worth her while with great, high-value treats and prevent her from becoming frustrated by all the displacements. You should make an effort to have everyone in the household randomly perform at least one or two of the exercises (including displacing the dog, approaching the location when the dog occupies it, and handling the dog when she is in the location) at least once weekly. In a household of three people, that would mean at least three to six exercises per week.

## Person Guarding

You may not think of your problem as guarding when the dog uses aggressive behavior to avoid having others approach or contact you. You may label it jealousy, but this label is not particularly helpful in suggesting the contingencies that maintain the actual behaviors. It would be more useful to view the behavior as similar to any situation in which the dog aggresses in order to keep others away from a valued resource. Person guarding is often maintained by negative reinforcement. That is, the aggressive behavior reliably results in others moving away, and this withdrawal (which is what the dog wants) makes the behavior more probable in the future. In some instances, guardians can accidentally maintain these behaviors through positive reinforcement. If you inadvertently reinforce the dog for aggressing—for example, by trying to calm the dog down or to avoid a conflict—the aggressive behaviors can increase in frequency as a result. That's why a proper contingency statement is necessary. Your actual behavior change program should be designed on the basis of that contingency statement. Knowing which form of reinforcement maintains the behavior can help with formulating a behavior change program.

This behavior has some common presentations. The provocative stimulus can be the approach of another person or another dog, or specifically physical contact. The dog will seek to split or otherwise separate the person she is guarding from the other person or dog. If aggressive behaviors successfully achieve this end, a problem is likely to develop.

There are many strategic approaches to this problem. In one, a more operant approach can be taken. This involves replacing the aggressive behaviors with an incompatible behavior, such as sitting patiently or making eye contact with the handler, rather than focusing on the other person or dog. Another approach is to shape prosocial encounters with the other person or dog, at gradually increasing levels of intensity. Alternatively, the focus can be more on a respondent approach. This involves systematically desensitizing the dog to the approach and contact of the other person or dog. I prefer to use a behavior replacement procedure, training the replacement behavior in a graded, incremental way (often involving shaping). This approach achieves both respondent and operant conditioning goals.

In any case, the procedure is similar to those used for the other forms of guarding described above. It involves starting with a rank-order list of the dog's top three reinforcers and a list in rank order of the situations that provoke aggressive behaviors. Knowing these will enable you to formulate a graded protocol in which incrementally greater intensities of the problem stimuli are presented at the same time as a replacement behavior is installed. The replacement behavior can be an incompatible, alternative or other behavior. Antecedent control procedures should also be used. For example, exercise and, in some cases, medication can change the dog's physiology so that training proceeds more easily. Tethering or use of a muzzle can be helpful for ensuring everyone's safety.

As before, the process entails presenting the stimulus at a level at which the dog is unlikely to behave aggressively, and heavily reinforcing the replacement behavior. Then the process is repeated with incremental increases in the intensity of the stimulus. The ultimate aim is to transfer stimulus control such that the dog performs the new behavior when presented with the problem stimulus.

## Predatory Behaviors

Predatory behavior, in which a dog behaves aggressively towards another animal that she sees as prey, are a combination of reflexes and operants. This behavior has a strong basis in the dog's genetic makeup, as opposed to being learned. However, just because a behavior is genetically based, "instinctive" or innate does not mean that it is not open to conditioning. Nevertheless, much of the reinforcement for predatory behaviors seems to be intrinsic or automatic, and this makes these behaviors difficult to manage effectively through behavior replacement.

An important part of managing predatory behaviors is to manipulate antecedents so that the dog is not stimulated to stalk and attack. Other aspects of management are solid verbal control and guardian vigilance. You should also train the dog in some basic behaviors such as coming when called (recall), sit and look (pay attention) to a high degree of reliability. As well as solid verbal control, the use of equipment such as muzzles and leashes will be very important.

It is possible to design protocols in which incompatible behaviors, such as recalls, are trained in the presence of the problem stimulus, using gradual increases in the intensity of the stimulus. In some cases, medications can help modify predatory behavior. However, the most common solutions to predatory aggression are antecedent control procedures, equipment use and solid verbal control.

## Dog–Dog Aggressive Behavior

Aggressive behaviors between dogs are often complex. It can be difficult to control the behavior of other dogs and hence to control the protocols. Effective change of the behavior will be less likely if the environment cannot be adequately controlled. There is also a significant risk of injury associated with dog–dog aggressive behaviors. You need to have realistic goals. If the dog is a hard biter (that is, she inflicts bites that cause nontrivial damage), then perhaps environmental management (antecedent control procedures) rather than active behavior change protocols is the best approach. These dogs may never be able to be fully trusted around other dogs, and the risk is significant both for them and for their victims. For dogs who are not hard biters, more options are available. Often, micromanagement is required, rather than just straightforward protocols based on respondent or operant procedures. Two great (must-read) books on dog–dog aggression are *Fight! A Practical Guide to the Treatment of Dog–Dog Aggression* by Jean Donaldson, and *Feeling Outnumbered? How to Manage and Enjoy Your Multi-Dog Household* by Karen London and Patricia McConnell.

In some cases, the dog seems to be what some might call a "bully," who uses intimidating behaviors with other dogs. Often, the conciliatory behavior of the other dog reinforces this kind of behavior. Remedial socialization and training the dog to walk away from other dogs on cue can be helpful in encouraging better social relations with other dogs. I would start these cases with an exercise program, neutering of the dog where appropriate, perhaps dietary changes, and training to increase the verbal control that you have over the dog under highly distracting environmental conditions. At the same time, you should manage the environment in order to prevent the dog from behaving aggressively. Once these interventions are well under way, remedial socialization and training protocols can begin.

Social rehabilitation or remedial socialization is all about improving the dog's social skills by carefully orchestrating social interactions between her (provided that she does not have a hard bite) and other dogs. The aggressive dog has probably learned that her intimidation tactics and aggressive behavior produce reinforcement, although there may also be a genetic component making the behavior an aspect of the dog's temperament. Whether she wants a resource or just the opportunity to intimidate, she has come to learn that these behaviors will be reinforced. The goal for social rehabilitation, then, is to allow the dog to learn different contingencies. This entails finding dogs who will provide such alternative contingencies. Rather than accepting the dog's challenges or bowing to intimidation, these dogs are highly socially competent. They are not fazed by a blustery dog or intimidated easily. They are socially oriented, use appropriate social signals to encourage play and do not give up easily. Some trainers call these "bombproof dogs." The dog to be enlisted for social rehabilitation should be the same size or slightly larger than the dog who uses aggressive behavior, not a much smaller dog. Even a bombproof dog who is half the size can be trampled or injured without a single bite taking place.

It can be very difficult to enlist volunteers for these exercises. Not many dogs fit the bill and, even if one is found, the dog's guardian has to be convinced to allow their dog to be used. Usually, only diehard dog-park visitors or those active in a canine sport or training club are able to find such dogs because they come into contact with numerous well-socialized dogs and their guardians. If you are not in a position to find and enlist such volunteers, that is fine, and other aspects of behavior change programming will be focused on instead.

It is essential that you are absolutely sure that your dog does not have a hard bite before even considering these exercises. If the dog has been in numerous scuffles but has never delivered a bite that broke skin, this is probably a good indication that the bite is soft and generally reliable. If the dog has bitten and broken skin (not just a scratch resulting from the other dog pulling away, but an actual puncture) then do not consider these exercises, as they are just too risky.

Some guidelines follow for social rehabilitation of dogs who are aggressively intimidating but have a history of softer bites and no hard bites. These play sessions should be performed immediately after a good exercise session, so that pent-up energy is not influencing the interactions but the positive mood-altering effects of exercise are. Much of the precautions presented here I learned from Jean Donaldson's wonderful books. These exercises should only be performed with the assistance of a professional animal behavior consultant.

- Do not have any toys present at first. Have on hand equipment for breaking up a fight in case you need it, including a loud air horn (or some stainless steel pots that can be banged together), and a large piece of plywood that may be inserted between the dogs to separate them. You will need at least two experienced dog people—people who understand dog interactions and will be prepared to separate the dogs if necessary. If there are more than two dogs in the session, you should have at least one person per dog. Use a secured place that is big enough that the dogs can manage their distance properly but not so big they can get far away from you (in case you need to intervene). A very large room or small yard is ideal. Ideally, it should not be the problem dog's home or yard because she will usually be less inhibited in familiar surroundings. If you use a room, the floor should not be slippery, so that the dogs have sure footing as they move about.

- Let the dogs go all at once without much fuss. The aggressor will probably barge right over to one of the other dogs, skip polite greeting rituals and either begin intimidating behaviors (such as repeatedly putting the chin or paw on the other dog's back or standing over them) or perhaps start right in with blustery behavior.

The bombproof dog will ideally ignore the blustery behavior and continue to encourage proper greeting rituals or solicit play. The bombproof dog's job is to discourage inappropriate behaviors and encourage appropriate ones. They are bombproof because they are not discouraged by crude or inappropriate behavior from other dogs and keep trying to interact with them in a normal social fashion. The hope is that the bombproof dog will manage to punish or extinguish inappropriate behaviors and reinforce appropriate behaviors with social play. Scuffles may break out. These can be a learning experience for the subject dog, teaching her that she cannot just push everyone else around without unpleasant consequences and that prosocial signals can result in fun and games.

- If a real fight breaks out, have the two most experienced people (agreed on beforehand) separate the dogs. The other people present should collect the other dogs so that they do not interfere with the fight or join in. Allow the dogs a couple of minutes to cool down apart, and then resume the play session. If the dogs continue to get into fights, you should separate them for a day or two in order to allow their body chemistry to return to normal, and then perhaps try again. If the aggressor is getting into repeated fights with one dog, it is probably best to remove that dog from the sessions. It is difficult to speculate on why two particular dogs may not get along, but repeated fights can undermine the rehabilitation efforts.

- If all goes relatively well, the dogs will play for a while, and you should ideally start to see signs that the rehabilitation is working (if not in the first session, then in later ones).

The above advice is, of course, only generic. A solid contingency statement is required in order to know what is maintaining the aggressive behaviors. There are many variables to consider in setting up and running these sessions, and experienced judgment and flexibility are necessary. You should always quantify the aggressive behaviors before, during and after this process. Here are some indications that progress is being made:

- increased frequency of nonaggressive social communication, including appropriate greeting rituals and tolerance of investigation and other behaviors from other dogs
- decreased frequency or intensity of fights.

In general, the more sessions such as these that can be arranged, the better. Each session should ideally end once the dogs have become bored with one another and are not playing together as much but rather sniffing around and exploring the environment more. Signs of improvement should be seen after a few sessions. If there is no improvement within, say, the first five sessions or so, the contingencies relating to the behavior are not being addressed adequately in the present arrangement. In this case, you may decide to drop the efforts towards social rehabilitation and focus on other aspects of managing the dog's behavior. If you do see improvement, the play sessions can continue, and you can experiment with adding in a few moderately valued toys if the aim is for the dog to handle real dog-park situations at some point.

Once things are going well, an "average" dog can be added to the mix. This should not be a dog who is particularly sensitive, but it can be one who is not as diplomatic as the bombproof dogs. Once that is going well, another average dog could perhaps be added.

At the same time as working on social rehabilitation, you should also be working on training between sessions. Once things are going well with the social rehabilitation sessions, the training can be applied during the social rehabilitation sessions, and then in other groups, such as at the dog-park or training club. When you move to "real world" settings, a couple of setbacks might occur at first as the dog generalizes the new lessons to another location and to new dogs. It is best to start at the new location when there is less activity at the park or club, or when mostly sturdy dogs will be present, and use management and careful awareness of what is going on to create an easier transition for the dog.

In the training part of the plan, we begin to use verbal control to intervene in situations that look volatile. The dog can be requested to back off. This should be done at first when the dog is in an interaction with another dog where it is likely that she will come away from the interaction on request. Usually this means at times that are not tense and usually near the end of a session. The cue word (such as "leave it") should be different from the recall command. Here are the steps:

- Deliver the cue, and then encourage (prompt) your dog to walk away from the other dog. You can clap the side of your leg or make some noises—whatever works. As soon as your dog steps away from the other dog, click and treat, allowing her to immediately return to whatever she wants to be doing. This only works if receiving the treat, with a short break in interacting with the other dog, is of higher value to the dog than continuing to interact.

- Repeat until the dog will step away from other dogs on cue without the other prompts.

- Require the dog to walk a few extra steps away from the other dog before you click and treat. Get it to the point where she will step away from dogs when requested and take several steps away.

- Start using the cue during slightly more distracting encounters. Repeat until it is solid.

- Start using the cue during more distracting and tense encounters. This includes situations in which the dog gets stuck in certain problematic behaviors when meeting another dog, such as remaining in an intimidating posture for more than a few seconds, placing her paw over the other dog, mounting the other dog or putting her chin on the other dog's shoulders. Avoid calling your dog away from an encounter when she is remaining still and the other dog is investigating her. In these situations, remaining still is the proper behavior; moving away, obeying you, could start a fight.

- You might find that the dog starts to disengage from encounters on her own, without the cue, after a bit of consistent work. If that happens, reinforce it, and always be on the lookout for it so that you can encourage it. This will mean that the situation itself is becoming the cue for the new behavior. If this does not happen, just continue to use the cue in order to cut off a tense encounter before it gets too tense. You do not want to be overprotecting, calling the dog away from all encounters, because you want her to learn prosocial ways to work with other dogs. On the other hand, when you know that an encounter is likely to go badly, use the cue early in the process before she performs the problem behaviors.

You should maintain progress by continuing regular socialization with other dogs, using antecedent control procedures to ward off high-risk encounters, and using your cue to have the dog disengage from problematic moments. If some aggression occurs on leash, the section above on behavior change options for on-leash aggressive behaviors is relevant.

Some dogs have problems with other dogs because they become easily aroused and have poor social skills, not because they tend to use a lot of intimidating behaviors. They are socially sloppy and fail to switch roles during play, or they come on too strong. In these cases, remedial socialization and solid verbal control are also appropriate.

When the dog makes use of extensive threat displays and uses aggressive signals only when cornered, a behavior replacement procedure with a graded incremental approach might be appropriate. This will ensure not only a replacement behavior but also counterconditioning. Along with the usual distance and duration variables that influence the intensity of exposure to the other dog, Donaldson (2004) suggests these additional variables:

- how passive the other dog is (the more passive, the easier to work with)
- size of the other dog (this can be specific to the dog who behaves aggressively, but often similar or slightly smaller dogs are easier for the dog to accept than larger ones)
- orientation of the other dog (the rear is less threatening than the front)
- number of dogs (generally, the fewer dogs present, the easier it is for the dog to accept).

Generally, protocols should be designed to manipulate distance incrementally as each of these variables is worked on. Often, more than one variable can be manipulated at the same time. How the dog responds will determine how many variables can be combined. For example, the protocol might start with a single, passive, smallish dog who is oriented away from the subject dog at 20 feet (or whatever the particular distance is that the dog can handle easily). At each step of the protocol, this dog gets closer and closer. The next step might be to start well back and have the other dog oriented toward rather than away from the subject dog. It might then be possible to do that run-through with a more active dog also oriented toward the subject dog. If this is too much, the orientation variable might be relaxed and the activity of the dog could be increased, with the dog facing away at this stage. Variables can be worked together where possible, but separated where necessary. The most important things are to avoid aggressive displays and not to move on to the next level of intensity until the one before is solid; ideally, the dog should also be showing a pleasure-related emotional response before you proceed to the next level.

In most cases, you should keep the dog on leash as a safety and management measure. If the aggressive behavior includes more extensive appeasement behavior and emotional responses, the same approach as for on-leash aggression can be used. The goal in this case is to train the dog to maintain eye contact with you when walking past another dog, to make an emergency U-turn when confronted by a surprise, or to sit-and-make-eye-contact when faced with an off-leash dog. Training the dog to carry out a specific task in the face of a confrontation instills confidence in the dog, who can focus on the task rather than on the other dog. On the other hand, many dogs do better when they are reinforced for paying nonaggressive attention to the problem dog. For these dogs, attending to something away from the other dog makes them more anxious. For details on training these behaviors, review the on-leash aggression section in this chapter. The best approach will depend on your goals and the particular problem contingencies.

Another common problem arising among dogs is resource guarding. In most cases, the frequency and magnitude of the aggressive displays do not tend to increase, and little or no damage is done. Whether you will need to, or choose to, intervene at all requires a judgment call. In many cases of resource guarding among dogs, an operant conditioning approach works well. This involves identifying an incompatible or alternative behavior to replace the aggressive behavior. One technique is to train the guarding dog to walk away from the other dog, bringing the resource with her, rather than remaining in the situation with it. The dog can also be trained to walk away and leave the resource with the other dog, although a high value reinforcer will have to be provided for this option. The dog should be set up for success by creative manipulation of the antecedents. The behavior change process involves minimizing aggressive displays, maximizing the opportunity for the dog to receive reinforcers for appropriate behavior, and building up gradually in intensity. The aim is for the dog to learn that the replacement behavior pays off better, as quickly and seamlessly as possible.

If the guarding dog is also showing emotional responses, respondent conditioning is needed as well as operant conditioning in the protocols. This will involve presenting the evoking stimulus (the other dog) in a graded, incremental way to ensure that problematic emotional responses and emotional behaviors are minimized. Then, desirable behaviors can be reinforced.

For this kind of problem, Jean Donaldson (2004) proposes a respondent approach very similar to these stages:

- Sitting dogs fed in sequence. Have two dogs tethered apart, give a treat to the other dog and then immediately praise and treat the guarder, repeating until the guarder is obviously pleased to see the other dog getting a treat.
- Decrease distance. Gradually have the dogs closer to one another while repeating the above steps.
- Entrances without resources present. Remain in a room with the tethered guarder, being generally boring for 20 minutes, with no valued resources present. Bring the other dog in on leash, have her

sit, treat her and then immediately praise and treat the guarder. Then remove the other dog and go back to being boring. Repeat until the guarder seems happy about entrance and treating of the other dog.

- Generalize the step above to other rooms. Repeat the process in some other rooms to ensure the response does not become specific to just one room.
- Entrances with low-value resource present. Repeat the process above, but this time allow the guarder to have a no-value or extremely low-value resource. Go slowly with this step. When the other dog comes in, you may have to ensure that she is not directly facing the guarder and that she is not allowed to approach the guarder too closely. Repeat the process, gradually working the distance and orientation variables.
- Entrances with higher value resource. Repeat the process, but this time with a slightly higher value resource. Remember to relax the orientation and distance variables and any other variables you discover are important and work up gradually.
- Entrances with high-value resources. Repeat the process, but this time with a highly valued resource.
- Entrances, guarder off tether, other dog on leash. For this run, repeat the process through low- to medium- and high-value resources, but with the guarder off tether. Remember to relax criteria such as distance and orientation and work up gradually.
- Entrances with eye contact. Repeat the process, but this time encourage the other dog to make eye contact with the guarder. If a solid emotional response has been installed, this should go smoothly, but remember to relax other variables and work up gradually. Eye contact is a major provocation, so work this stage intensively.
- Generalize. Repeat the process in other rooms to ensure that the emotional response does not become specific to a particular location but generalizes to other locations.
- Other dog off leash. Use a low-value resource and repeat the process, this time with the other dog off leash. Ensure that the other dog is suitable for these tasks and is not likely to charge right over to the guarder, and is not a resource guarder herself. Gradually increase the value of the resource used.
- Generalize. Generalize the conditioning to other rooms.
- Cold trials. Try the exercises in what seems more like a real-life event, rather than in a session of repeated exercises. Of course, you control the value of the resources present and the type of dog you use, to set the guarder up for success, but these should appear more like real-life single events to the guarder.

- Continue to maintain the conditioned response by repeating the cold trials from time to time.

## Dog–Dog Aggressive Behavior Between Dogs who Live Together

Aggressive behaviors between dogs who live together are often associated with female dogs, whereas aggressive behaviors between dogs who do not live together are often associated with intact male dogs. Intact male dogs should be neutered, as this can reduce aggressive behavior in some cases. Karen London and Patricia McConnell wrote a terrific book called *Feeling Outnumbered? How to Manage and Enjoy Your Multi-Dog Household*, in which they outline a basic strategy for working with dog-aggressive dogs who live together. London and McConnell (2001) were among the first to abandon the outdated practice of "supporting the hierarchy" (that is, giving preferential treatment to the dog who seems to be the "top dog"). Instead, they outline an operant conditioning approach that has proven very successful. This general approach is outlined below as it is the approach I take as well. If you have a problem with fighting between your household dogs, I strongly suggest you read London and McConnell's book.

### *Train Each Dog Individually*

The dogs who are fighting should be separated, at the very least when they are not supervised. This and other management practices will break the cycle of habitual aggressive encounters. You can then start working on individual training of each dog and solid verbal control. You should arrange to have time alone with each dog for training. This should be a pleasant time, and can incorporate walks and play sessions or exercise sessions as well as training. It should be made into a real bonding time. When a bunch of dogs is running around all the time, it is easy for the dogs to get used to not paying attention to people because your attention is usually divided. You must train each dog individually to a high level of reliability, in basic control cues that will allow you to verbally control each dog. The training will also teach the dog to be patient and show impulse control.

It is easy to train a dog to come when called or sit when asked, but will the dog come away from playing with another dog or from a tense encounter with another dog? If not, then you need to train the behaviors further. The basic responses of "leave it," "here," "sit" and "down" should be practiced until the dog will perform them under high levels of distraction. The more individual training sessions you put in, and the more reliable the responses are in varied environments, the more effective the behavior change program will be.

## Train in Pairs

Once you are at a reliable point in individual training, you will start training the dogs in pairs, even if you have several dogs. The training involves reinforcing each dog for tolerating attention paid to the other dog. Cue the dogs to sit, using the name of each dog before the cue, so that they know that the cue is for them. Then release and treat one dog, and then the other. This training should start when both dogs are receptive, and with the dogs far enough away from each another that they are not aggressing. Once you have worked with one pair, you can work with another pair if you have more than two dogs. You can start with the easy dogs and work your way up to more difficult ones. If it is only one dog who is the main problem, the focus should be on that one, but you should still perform the training with each pair combination.

You can also work on group commands, using a group name such as "everyone," followed by the cue. Only those dogs who perform the behavior are treated. This group command will come in handy when you want all the dogs to respond to a cue. "Sit" delivered to all dogs at once, for instance, can be valuable.

## Train in Groups

Once you have worked your way through training each pair combination to a reliable level of distraction, you can start combinations of three dogs. The training will proceed in much the same way as with pairs; that is, with the dogs at a distance from each other, and working with each dog in turn. Once significant progress has been made in these small groups in each possible combination of three, you can start adding in any other dogs within the household, until you have your whole group working together. You should maintain the training by continuing to work with the dogs individually and as a group, and applying the training to everyday life when possible.

# RECOMMENDED RESOURCES

## Books

*The Culture Clash* by Jean Donaldson (the greatest dog book ever written).
*Mine! A Practical Guide to Resource Guarding in Dogs* by Jean Donaldson.
*Fight! A Practical Guide to the Treatment of Dog–Dog Aggression* by Jean Donaldson.
*How Dogs Learn* by Mary Burch and Jon Bailey (more details on how dogs learn).
*Feisty Fido: Help for the Leash-Aggressive Dog* by Patricia McConnell and Karen London.
*Feeling Outnumbered? How to Manage and Enjoy Your Multi-Dog Household* by Karen London and Patricia McConnell.
*The Power of Positive Dog Training* by Pat Miller.
*Don't Shoot the Dog! The New Art of Teaching and Training* by Karen Pryor.
*Help for Your Fearful Dog* by Nicole Wilde.

## Web Sites

International Institute for Applied Companion Animal Behavior
http://www.IIACAB.com

International Association of Animal Behavior Consultants
http://www.IAABC.org

Association of Pet Dog Trainers
http://www.APDT.com

Companion Animal Sciences Institute (distance learning)
http://www.CASInstitute.com

Academy for Dog Trainers (hands on, on site)
http://www.sfspca.org/academy/

Certificate IV in Companion Animal Services (Australian)
http://www.deltasocietyaustralia.com.au/canine_good_citizens_instructor s_course.htm

# GLOSSARY OF TERMS

**Affiliative Signals**. Affiliative signals function to promote friendly, cooperative social encounters between individuals who are meeting for the first time, or to provide recognition and continued affiliation for those in established relationships. They usually serve an approach/contact function. Contrast with *Agonistic Signals*.

**Aggression**. For the purposes of this workbook, aggression is defined as "attacks, attempted attacks or threats of attack by one individual directed at another individual." Structurally, threat or attack behavior. In dogs, this usually refers to snarling, growling, lunging, snapping and biting. Functionally, aggression is threat or attack behavior that functions to achieve access to a stimulus, or escape from or avoidance of a stimulus.

**Aggressive Signals**. Communication signals involving a threat of attack. A type of agonistic signal, the other type being appeasement signals. See *Aggression* and *Agonistic Signals*.

**Agonistic Signals**. Includes attack, escape, threat, defense, and appeasement behaviors. Contrast with *Affiliative Signals*.

**Antecedent**. Conditions present prior to the behavior in question. Antecedents that influence operant behavior are generally divided into three categories: setting events, motivating operations and discriminative stimuli. They each contribute to how likely a behavior is to occur.

**Antecedent Control Procedure**. Any procedure that manipulates antecedents in order to increase or decrease the likelihood of a target operant behavior. This involves changes to discriminative stimuli, motivating operations, setting events or response effort.

**Arousal**. Activation of the nervous system generally. Stimulates action, or even inaction.

**Aversive Stimulus**. A stimulus that an organism acts to evade, escape from, or avoid. Aversive stimulation can result in some problematic secondary effects, such as aggression, countercontrol, social disruption and emotional escape/avoidance behavior. Aversive stimulation involves fear- or pain-eliciting stimuli.

**Chaining** (or Behavior Chaining). A procedure in which an animal is trained to perform a chain of behaviors in sequence. Each behavior provides the cue for the next behavior, and only the last behavior in the chain results in delivery of a primary reinforcer.

**Conditioned Emotional Response**. Form of conditioned response whereby emotional reactions such as fear, anger or joy are elicited.

**Contingency**. In respondent conditioning, contingency refers to a positive correlation between the conditioned stimulus and the unconditioned stimulus. In operant conditioning, it refers to a relationship between an operant and a consequence, in which the consequence occurs if, and only if, the operant occurs. Generally, it refers to the relationship between a behavior and its controlling environmental variables.

**Contingency Statement**. A concise statement of a particular behavior problem, identifying the behavior in question as well as its antecedents and maintaining consequences. It is constructed based on a functional assessment.

**Counterconditioning**. A respondent conditioning process in which the animal's previous conditioned response to a stimulus is changed or reversed with new conditioning. In most cases, counterconditioning is used to change a conditioned emotional response from fearful to joyful, or anxiety to relaxation. It is the principle underlying systematic desensitization.

**Discriminative Stimulus**. An antecedent stimulus that indicates that a specific contingency is in effect. Saying "sit" indicates to a dog that, if they sit now, some given schedule of reinforcement will be in effect. When the word "sit" is not given, this contingency is not in effect.

**Empowerment**. A state of confidence in one's ability to operate on one's environment effectively and to create reinforcing contingencies. While empowerment is conducive to psychological wellbeing, learned helplessness is its antithesis.

**Fear**. An emotional response, involving both operants and respondents, characterized by signs of sympathetic nervous system arousal, stress, and escape or avoidance behaviors.

**Free-Shaping**. A training procedure in which successive approximations to a terminal behavior are reinforced. Successive approximations to the terminal behavior are captured; that is, the trainer does not prompt responses, but rather waits for the approximation and provides reinforcement when it occurs. Once the approximation is stable, a closer approximation is required for reinforcement. This continues until the terminal behavior is achieved.

**Frustration**. Emotional behavior resulting from being blocked from achieving one's goals. Frustration can precipitate aggressive responses.

**Functional Assessment**. Term used to describe a range of evaluation strategies and techniques, all geared to identifying the ABCs of a behavior.

**Learned Helplessness**. When an animal is exposed to uncontrollable and severe aversive stimulation, they will frequently abandon efforts to escape or avoid it and will not be able to learn escape or avoidance behaviors, even when these options become readily available. Learning is inhibited, and behavior tends to be suppressed.

**Negative Punishment**. A procedure in which a behavior results in the withdrawal of a stimulus and, as a result, future frequency of that behavior decreases. It is also a basic principle of behavior.

**Negative Reinforcement**. A procedure in which a behavior results in the withdrawal of a stimulus and, as a result, future frequency of that behavior increases. It is also a basic principle of behavior.

**Operant**. Behavior that operates on the environment to produce consequences. Goal-directed behavior.

**Operant Conditioning**. A change (increase or decrease) in the frequency of an operant as a function of its consequences.

**Positive Punishment**. A procedure in which a behavior results in the presentation of a stimulus and, as a result, future frequency of that behavior decreases. It is also a basic principle of behavior.

**Positive Reinforcement**. A procedure in which a behavior results in the presentation of a stimulus and, as a result, future frequency of that behavior increases. It is also a basic principle of behavior.

**Prosocial**. Friendly or otherwise seeking an approach or contact function.

**Reinforcement**. Increase in the future frequency of a behavior resulting from it's consequences.

**Respondent**. An unconditioned response (reflex) or conditioned response that is elicited by a stimulus (unconditioned or conditioned).

**Respondent Conditioning**. Occurs when a neutral stimulus is paired with a stimulus that elicits a reflexive response. After conditioning has occurred, the neutral stimulus itself elicits the same type of response. How we make previously meaningless stimuli elicit reflexive behaviors.

**Shaping**. A process whereby successive approximations to a target behavior are reinforced in increments until that target behavior (called the terminal behavior) is achieved. The behavior may be captured as it occurs or prompted. See also *Free-Shaping*.

**Stimulus**. A thing or event that can influence behavior.

**Systematic Desensitization**. A procedure, usually involving deep relaxation training; construction of a hierarchy of stimuli that elicit fear, anxiety or phobia; and counterconditioning through the hierarchy.

# REFERENCES CITED

Bradley, J. (2005). *Dogs bite: But balloons and slippers are more dangerous.* Berkeley: James & Kenneth.

Bradley, J. (2006). *Dog bites: Problems and solutions.* (Policy paper). Baltimore: The Animals and Society Institute.

Donaldson, J. (1996). *The culture clash.* Oakville, Ontario: James and Kenneth.

Donaldson, J. (1998). *Dogs are from Neptune.* Montreal, Canada: Lasar Multimedia Productions.

Donaldson, J. (2002). *Mine! A practical guide to resource guarding in dogs.* San Francisco: San Francisco SPCA.

Donaldson, J. (2004). *Fight! A practical guide to the treatment of dog–dog aggression.* San Francisco: San Francisco SPCA.

Kalnajs, S. (2006). *Language of dogs* (DVD): Blue Dog Training & Behavior. Produced by Media Paws.

London, K. B., & McConnell, P. B. (2001). *Feeling outnumbered? How to manage and enjoy your multi-dog household.* Black Earth: Dog's Best Friend, Ltd.

McConnell, P. B., & London, K. B. (2003). *Feisty Fido: Help for the leash-aggressive dog.* Black Earth: Dog's Best Friend, Ltd.

Phillips, K. (2005). *Avoiding liability when you train, shelter or adopt-out.* Seminar and essential legal documents (DVD and CD).

Pryor, K. (1999). *Don't shoot the dog! The new art of teaching and training.* New York: Bantam Books.

Pryor, K. (2002). *Getting started: Clicker training for dogs* (New expanded ed.). Waltham: Sunshine Books, Inc.

Sidman, M. (2000). *Coercion and its fallout* (Revised ed.). Boston: Author's Cooperative, Inc. Publishers.

Sorenson, S. (2002). Serotonin syndrome. *Utox Update, A Publication of the Utah Poison Control Center for Health Professionals, 4(4),* 1–2.